images

The Best of British Illustration

acknowledgements

The AOI would like to thank:
All the Images 18 judges listed in the sections of this annual.
Gina Morley – *Chief Administrator*
Heather McDonough – *Exhibition and print coordinator*
Sue Christie – *Financial Manager*
Claire Mackenzie – *Ex Chief Administrator*
The AOI Council: Gale Pitt, Michael Bramman, Margaret Wellbank,
Simon Farr, Ruth Gladwin, Pauline Hazelwood.

Very special thanks to Libby Drury at Still Price Lintas Advertising Agency for hosting the
book launch and exhibition.

The publisher is hugely indebted to the few unfeasibly gifted starlets who produced this
superb source book in around 6 weeks: Eva & Eugenie on sales, Cath inputs copy & edits,
Glenn & Tony design to unrealistic deadlines with some style & Gina, Heather & Sue at the
AOI generally suffer stoically with remarkably good humour.

Thanks too to Creative Review for sponsoring awards and Benson & Hedges for a good
quality smoke. Bulldog font kindly supplied by Clubtype Limited

Finally, a monster thanks to all the illustrators who by entering the competition and
investing in their own talent in the Professional & Newcomers sections, make *Images* the
highest quality illustrators' source book on the planet. May you be justly rewarded with
fame & fortune.

Publisher: David O'Sullivan, Trojan Horse Publishing

Sales: Eva Zwil & Eugenie Arrowsmith

Editor: Cath Campbell

Design: Cactus

Administration: Gina Morley, Heather McDonough, Sue Christie

Cover Illustration: By Ian Craig, *Commissioned by Decca records*

Warehousing & distribution: Ron Philpott

Retail sales & distribution: Art Books International London SW8 4UD

Colour Reproduction: Trinity Graphic Co. Ltd. Hong Kong

Print: L Rex Printing Co. Ltd. Hong Kong

Trojan Horse Publishing
1 Church Crescent
London E9 7DH
ISBN 0 9520326 1 9

contents

images

The Best of British Illustration

introduction

Now in its eighteenth year, the Images competition, exhibition and annual remains the major event showcasing the work of illustrators working in Britain.

The seven categories in the winners section of the book showcase the work selected by the 35 judges from the many hundreds of entrants to the competition. The judging panels are changed every year to ensure the inevitably subjective job of choosing the 'best' work does not result in the same names arising from year to year. The focus of Images is very much on presenting new ideas and trends in illustration amongst work of the highest calibre.

For the illustrators, the primary function of the Images annual is to promote their work to commissioning sources. The Association of Illustrators wholeheartedly supports this objective with the production of the annual by Trojan Horse Publishing at a minimum cost to the illustrators presenting their work.

Images 17 was extremely successful in this respect with many illustrators reporting the annual as their most lucrative source of commissions. With Images 18, the publisher is increasing free nationwide distribution to 3000 as well as moving into Europe and the United States with the aim of improving on last years 7000 total production.

The number and quality of illustrators showing has increased this year complemented by improvements in the annuals' usebility. The ultimate goal of the Images annual and competition is to provide illustrators with the maximum possible exposure for their work, whilst providing commissioners with a fresh and ever improving source of artists. With Images 18 we're well on the way to achieving that goal.

The AOI is governed by an annually elected Council of 6 members along with a full-time administrator and financial manager supported by a special promotions officer and numerous volunteers. Now firmly established at 29 Bedford Square, in company with the Chartered Society of Designers, the organisation looks forward to an ever more effective role as the sole body representing and promoting the interests of illustrators within the communications industry.

Illustration by Fletcher Sibthorp

part 1

The editorial section was judged by:

Cath Caldwell
Art Director - Elle magazine

Rami Lippa
Deputy Creative Director -
Redwood Publishing

Ursula Morgan
Art Director - Design Week

Sue Munrow Smith
Art Editor - VNU Publications

Chris Thurston
Art Director - Woman's Weekly

winners

Brian Cronin

fax: OlO 3531 280 7178   **tel: OlO 3531 280 76ll**

Montmolin
Royal Terrace Lane
Dunlaoghaire
County Dublin
Ireland

Title: Nomad's Land

Medium: Watercolour, pen & ink

Purpose of Work: Magazine illustration

Brief: To portray the cultural and philosophical changes brought about by the new mobile technology without illustrating the equipment itself

Commissioned by: Rami Lippa *Intercity*

Bee Willey

studio tel: 071 375 0323   fax: 071 375 0323

32 Grove Road
London E3 5AX

tel: 081 981 4900
fax: 081 980 4471

Purpose of Work: Magazine illustration

Commissioned by:
Elite Magazine (Germany)

I do a lot of work for magazines in Switzerland and France and would like to develop my work abroad, being fluent in German and half French

Much of my present work is for childrens' books, another development in the last two years

Michael Sheehy

tel: **081 693 4315**   fax: **081 693 4315**

115 Crystal Palace Road
East Dulwich
London
SE22 9ES

Title: Tradition versus Modernity

Medium: Mixed media

Purpose of Work: Magazine article

Brief: In the literary world, war is raging between the traditional men of letters and the deconstruction theorists

Commissioned by: *The Times Saturday Review*

Michael Sheehy

tel: **081 693 4315**   fax: **081 693 4315**

115 Crystal Palace Road
East Dulwich
London
SE22 9ES

Title: Food Pollution

Medium: Mixed media

Purpose of Work: Magazine article

Brief: Dirty soil, air and water are leading to the contamination of British fruit and vegetable crops

Commissioned by: Redwood Publishing

Client: *BBC Vegetarian Good Food Magazine*

11

Jamel Akib

fax: **0702 712899**   tel: **0702 712899**

32 Fernleigh Drive
Leigh-on-sea
Essex SS9 1LN

Medium: Pastel

Purpose of Work: Magazine illustration

Brief: To illustrate article on food safety

Commissioned by: Simon Rees *BBC Good Food* magazine,
Redwood Publishing

12

Christopher Gunson

tel: **071 622 7559**

63 Sudbury Court
Allen Edwards Drive
London SW8

Title: Mood Indigo

Medium: Acrylic

Purpose of Work: Magazine article

Brief: To illustrate the diagnosis of
Seasonal Affective Disorder (SAD)

Commissioned by: Juliet Brightmore *Jermyn Publications Ltd.*

Nancy Tolford

tel: **071 837 0509 / 071 254 3808** fax: **071 837 0509**

Studio 310
Panther House
38 Mount Pleasant
London WC1X OAP

Title: New Age Computing

Medium: Collage

Purpose of Work: Magazine article

Brief: The article discusses new computer programmes available for casting horoscopes, assessing biorhythms, relaxation techniques etc

Commissioned by: Rob Croty *VNU Publications*

Nancy Tolford

tel: **071 837 0509 / 071 254 3808** fax: **071 837 0509**

Studio 310
Panther House
38 Mount Pleasant
London WC1X OAP

Title: Time

Medium: Collage

Purpose of Work: Magazine article

Brief: Our traditional attitudes to time management need rethinking

Commissioned by: Steve Devane *Director Magazine*

Robin Harris

tel: **081 748 5998**

60 Weltje Road
London
W6 9L7

Title: Dancing with Death

Medium: Acrylic

Purpose of Work: Magazine article

Brief: To illustrate a text, being neither too comic or too grim, which described the demands made on a ballerina whereby she must adopt a lifestyle bordering on anorexic

Commissioned by: Graham Mitchener
The Observer Magazine

Fletcher Sibthorp

tel: **071 924 2473**

134 Salcott Road
London
SW11 6DG

Title: Ghost

Medium: Pastel & oil on canvas

Purpose of Work: Magazine article

Brief: To illustrate a text about relatives witnessing ghostly apparitions of recently-dead relatives

Commissioned by: Alison Pincott *GQ Magazine*

Tony McSweeney

tel: 071 403 1337   fax: 071 403 1337

1 Cathedral Street
London
SE1 9DE

Title: Je suis Myope

Medium: Pen, ink & watercolour

Purpose of Work: Newspaper article

Brief: To illustrate a text highlighting the lack of language skills in the British business community

Commissioned by: Ian Stupples *The Times*

Penny Sobr

tel: **071 240 5585**

2nd floor
6 Henrietta Street
London WC2E 8PR

Title: A Girl's Breast Friend

Medium: Gouache & ink

Purpose of Work: Magazine article

Brief: If the cup fits, wear it: most women buy the wrong size bra, which can lead to health problems. This was also a guide to fitting the right bra

Commissioned by: Mary Comber
Health & Fitness Magazine

Greg Becker

tel: **081 693 6120**

East Dulwich
London SE22 9DE

Title: Beyond Cosmic Ripples

Purpose of Work: Magazine article

Brief: It concerns the organisation of matter within the Universe and means of detecting it

Commissioned by: Colin Brewster *New Scientist*

Greg Becker

41 Whately Road
East Dulwich
London SE22 9DE

tel: **081 693 6120**

Title: A Smart House That Does Everything

Medium: Watercolour

Purpose of Work: Magazine illustration

Brief: Can computer technology be applied to everything? Or are intelligent houses - using robot cleaners, remote control wardrobes - just a quirky fad?

Commissioned by: Jo Dale *Independent on Sunday*

Sue Evans - Ffoto Fictions **tel: 0222 228367**

8 Wells Street
Riverside
Cardiff
CF1 8DW

Title: The Nosy Parkers

Purpose of Work:
Magazine article A Doctor Writes

Brief: To illustrate the confidentiality, or otherwise, of medical records

Commissioned by: Graham Mitchener *The Observer Magazine*

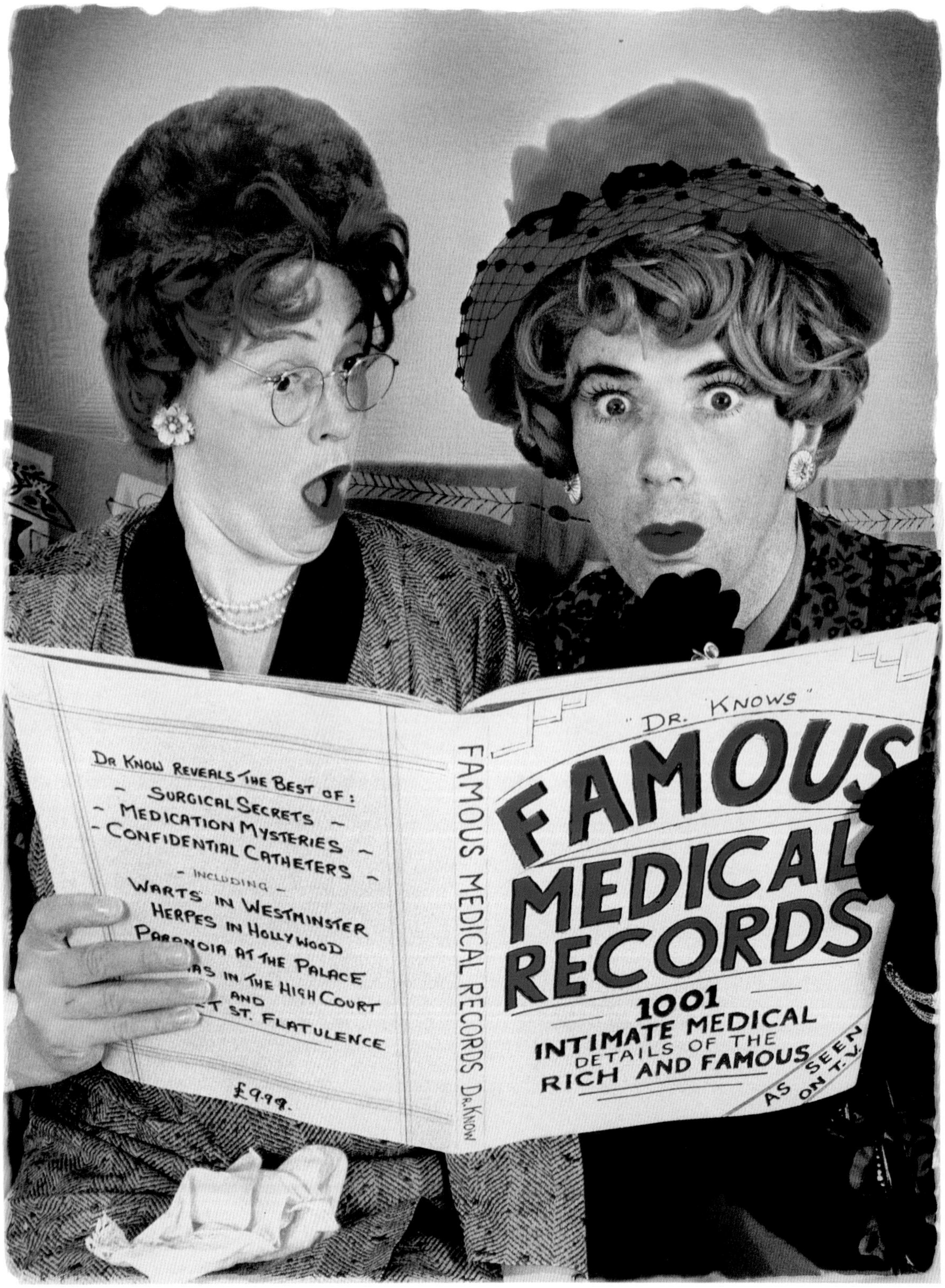

Ellis Nadler

tel: **071 388 5391**   fax: **071 387 6173**

PO Box 4DY
London W1A 4DY

Title: The Psychology of Lawns

Medium: Marker & ink

Purpose of Work: Magazine illustration

Brief: Does the state of your lawn reflect your personality?

Simon Fell

tel: **081 994 6206**   fax: **081 994 6206**

87 Rothschild Road
London
W4 5NT

Title: Staff Motivation

Medium: Colour copy & acrylics

Purpose of Work: Magazine article

Brief: Companies face a flood of departures unless they find ways other than money to keep staff happy

Commissioned by: Tracy Lingwood & Rob Croty *VNU Publications*

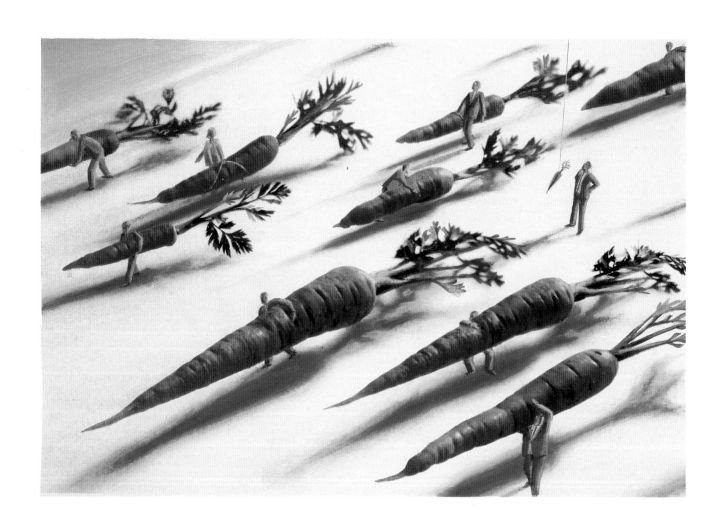

Simon Fell

tel: 081 994 6206   fax: 081 994 6206

87 Rothschild Road
London
W4 5NT

Title: The Tax Maze

Medium: Photocopy & watercolour

Purpose of Work: Magazine illustration

Brief: To depict the period after someone qualifies as a doctor but before they join a practice, when their tax and insurance position is complex and ambiguous

Commissioned by: Julian Cresswell *Morgan Grampian*

Ashley Potter

tel: **071 639 9695**

23 Collinson House
Peckham Park Road
London
SE15 6UU

Title: Drunk at Dinner

Medium: Acrylic

Brief: To depict moments of social embarrassment and faux pas

Commissioned by: Carolin Brügemann
Weiner Magazine

See Images 7 - 15

Geoff Grandfield

tel: **071 241 1523**

75 Church Walk
London
N16 8QR

Title: Letters from a Lost Horizon

Medium: Chalk pastel

Purpose of Work: Editorial

Brief: To illustrate an article by
Malise Ruthven reviewing a biography
of the travel writer Freya Stark

Commissioned by: Richard Gott *The Guardian*

Chris Burke

tel: 0892 531329

76 Auckland Road
Tunbridge Wells
Kent
TN1 7HS

Title: Politics in the Arts

Medium: Mixed

Purpose of Work: Newspaper illustration

Brief: To accompany an article deliberating whether peoples' political opinions are governed by their artistic abilities

Commissioned by: Lucy Pidduck *The Sunday Times*

Rebecca Gibbon

tel: **071 613 2323**   fax: **071 613 2726**

c/o The Inkshed
98 Columbia Road
London
E2 7QB

Title: Cancer

Medium: Watercolour

Purpose of Work: Editorial for Horoscope column

Bekah O'Neill

tel: **071 837 2931**

25 Ampton Street
London
WC1X 0LT

Agent: Folio
10 Gate Street
Lincoln's Inn Fields
London WC2A 3HP

tel: 071 242 9562   fax: 071 242 1816

Title: Potholes

Medium: Collage

Purpose of Work: Magazine Illustration

Brief: 'For most of us, potholes represent nothing more than a minor headache. For some, they lead to endless heartache and ruined lives'

Commissioned by: Terry Hawes
Boardroom Magazine

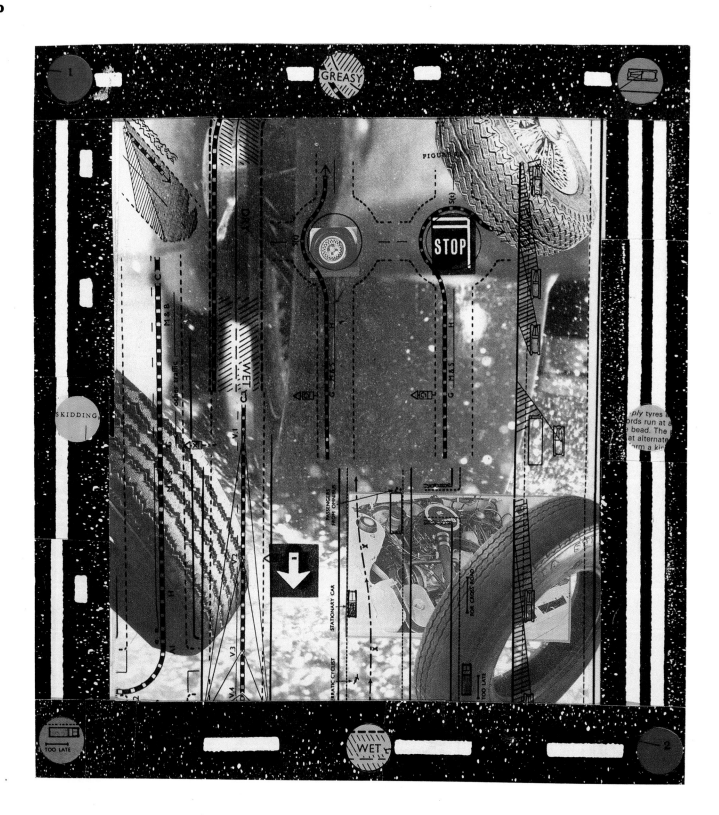

Ian Pollock

tel: **0625 426205**   fax: **0625 500617**

14 Crompton Road
Maccelsfield
Cheshire
SK11 8DS

Title: Lying Waste

Medium: Watercolour, ink and gouache

Commioned by:
Julia Worth, *BBC Good Food*

Ten million hens have been slaughtered and thousands of farmers have gone bankrupt, yet more people than ever are suffering from Salmonella poisoning

Grizelda Holderness

tel: **0452 740359**

Parks Cottage
The Green
Frampton-on-Severn
Glos.
GL2 7DU

Title: The Keeper

Medium: Pastel

Purpose of Work:
Illustration for a book review

Brief: To illustrate a review of two books concerning population and the environment: global collapse or a sustainable future?

Commissioned by: John Morris *The Times Saturday Review*

The book section was judged by:

Hilary Arnold
Publishing Director Studio Editions

Tony Lancaster
Creative Group Head - Book Club Associates

Alison Fenton
Children's Art Editor

Glen Savile
Senior Designer Pan Macmillan

David Fielder
Director - Sadie Fields

winners

Book
Advertising
Print & Design
Information & Technology
Unpublished Student
Unpublished Professional
Newcomers

Kevin Hauff

tel: **081 423 6486**

99 Tregenna Avenue
South Harrow
Middlesex
HA2 8QP

Agent: **Stephen Wells**
PO Box 651
London SE25 5PS

tel: **081 683 0607**
fax: **081 689 1427**

Title: Key Head

Medium: Acrylic

Purpose of Work:
Editorial illustration

Brief: To illustrate an article ('Safe and Sound'),which outlines ways of ensuring oneself against accidents, sickness and redundancy and of ways for homeowners to safeguard their property

Commissioned by: Will Atkins *Brass Tacks Publishing*

Philip Thompson

tel: 071 221 1925   fax: 071 243 0868

35 Elgin Crescent
London
W11 2JD

Title: The Bus Conductor Hines

Medium: Gouache

Purpose of Work: Book jacket

Commissioned by: Nikolaus Boulting *Orion Publishing*

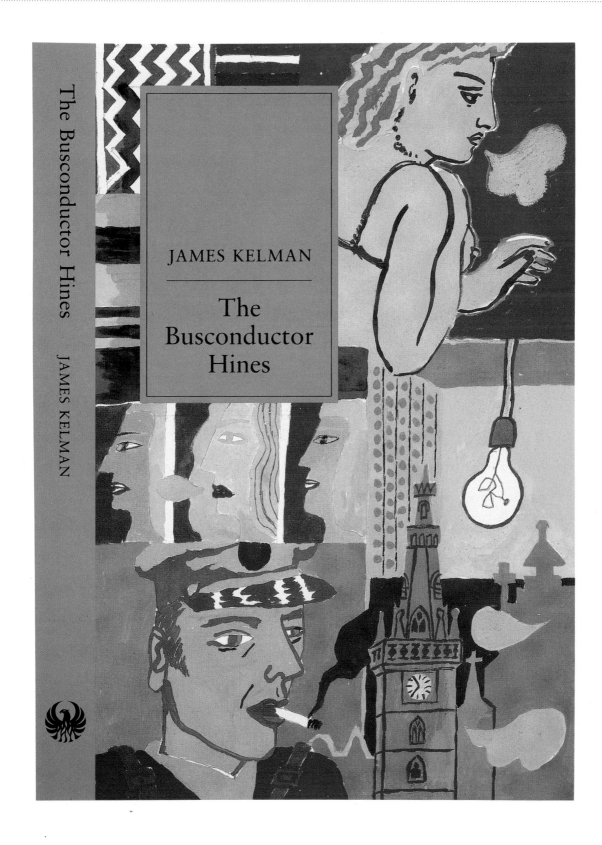

Toni Hargreaves

tel: 0772 253141   **fax: 0772 253141**

24 Warwick Road
Walton le Dale
Preston
Lancs
PR5 4GA

Title: Natureplay - Woods and Forests

Medium: Gouache

Purpose of Work: Childrens' book

Brief: To show seeds and fruits produced by trees being eaten by animals to aid seed dispersal

Commissioned by: Cathy Jones *Victoria House Publishing Ltd.*

36

Chris Burke

tel: **0892 531329**

76 Auckland Road
Tunbridge Wells
Kent
TN1 7HS

Title: Scraredy Cat

Medium: Mixed

Purpose of Work: Childrens' book

Brief: To interpret the text

Commissioned by: Janice English / Helen Diamond
Harcourt Brace / Collins Educational

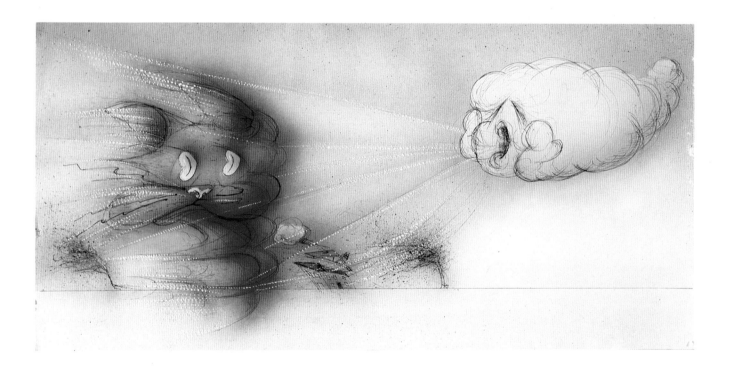

Paul Campion

tel: **0202 317014**   fax: **0202 317014**

Room C2
Ellerslie Chambers
2 Hinton Road
Bournemouth
Dorset BH1 2EF

Agent: Folio

tel: 071 636 9851

Title: Voice of Evil

Medium: Acrylic

Purpose of Work:
Childrens' paperback book cover

Brief: To produce an eyecatching and frightening representational image of the book

Commissioned by: Krystyna Zukonska *Boxtree Ltd.*

Paul Campion

tel: **0202 317014**   fax: **0202 317014**

Room C2
Ellerslie Chambers
2 Hinton Road
Bournemouth
Dorset BH1 2EF

Agent: Folio

tel: 071 636 9851
fax: 071 242 1816

Title: Knots and Crosses

Medium: Acrylic

Purpose of Work:
Paperback book cover

Brief: To produce an eyecatching
representational image of the book

Commissioned by: Ian Hughes
Coronet Books (Hodder & Staunton)

Malcolm Ashman

tel: **0225 312700**

21 Victoria Terrace
Bath
Avon
BA2 3QZ

Title: The Princess and The Dragon

Medium: Gouache

Purpose of Work:
To illustrate a story from a book of fairy tales.

Commissioned by: Pippa Rubenstein *Dragon's World*

Carolyn Gowdy

tel: **071 731 5380**

2C Maynard Close
(off Cambria Street)
London
SW6 2EN

Title: The Laughter of Heroes

Medium: Mixed

Purpose of Work: Book cover

Brief: To illustrate a bittersweet comedy about AIDS whereby a friend's illness forces a group of people to evaluate their own aches and longings

Commissioned by: Peter Ayrton *Serpent's Tail*

Jonathan Neale

The Laughter of Heroes

Destination : Dream of a Lifetime

'As satisfactorily wish-fulfilling as…Armistead Maupin'.
Patrick Gale

James Marsh

tel: 071 622 9530   **fax: 071 498 6851**

21 Elms Road
London
SW4 9ER

Title: More Haste Less Speed

Medium: Acrylic

Purpose of Work: Book illustration

Brief: An illustration for a proposed book on proverbs

James Marsh

tel: 071 622 9530   fax: 071 498 6851

21 Elms Road
London
SW4 9ER

Title: Kill not the Goose...

Medium: Acrylic

Purpose of Work: Book illustration

Brief: Illustration for a proposed book on proverbs

Peter Gudynas

tel: **021 459 0080**   fax: **021 459 0080**

89 Hazlewell Crescent
Stirchley
Birmingham
B30 2QE

Title: Entoverse

Purpose of Work: Cover for cybertext novel

Brief: To interpret themes concerned with virtual reality - representing artificially intelligent entity simulated within a computer-generated data space matrix universe

Commissioned by: Alan Lynch Artists New York USA

Client: *Ballantine Books* New York USA

44

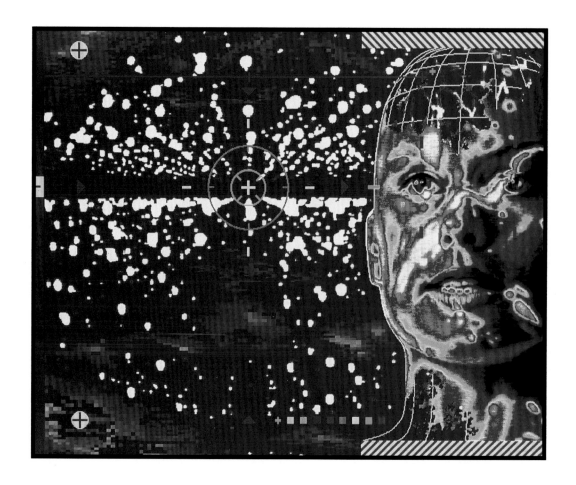

The advertising section was judged by:

Sally Bide
Art Buyer - BMPDDB Needham

Mark Dudley
Barraclough Hall Woolston

Peter McDermott
Creative Director - Team Advertising

winners

Book

Advertising

Print & Design

Information & Technology

Unpublished Student

Unpublished Professional

Newcomers

Graham Evans

tel: **071 240 8925** fax: **071 836 1177**

Agent:
Central Illustration Agency
36 Wellington Street
London
WC2E 7BD

Title: Honey

Medium: Collage & mixed media

Purpose of Work: Poster campaign to promote honey products

Brief: To create a summery, bright, uplifting graphic emphasising the bee and flowers, thus indicating the natural ingredients in the product

Commissioned by: Frances Myers (Art Director) *The Body Shop*

Andrew Harris

8A Birdhurst Rise
South Croydon
Surrey
CR2 7ED

tel: **081 681 0310**   fax: **081 681 0310**

Title: Keep the Volume Down

Medium: Lino-cut collage

Purpose of Work:
Posters for Underground

Brief: To promote a bold image reminding people not
to be inconsiderate with their personal stereos

Commissioned by: Malcolm Slater
The Jaffe Design Company

Client: London Underground

David McKean

Ebony Oast
Stone-cum-Ebony
Tenterden
Kent TN30 7HY

fax: **0797 270030**

Title: Cages: Heaven and Hell

Medium: Mixed

Purpose of Work: To advertise my own comic book series

Commissioned by: Kitchen Sink Press

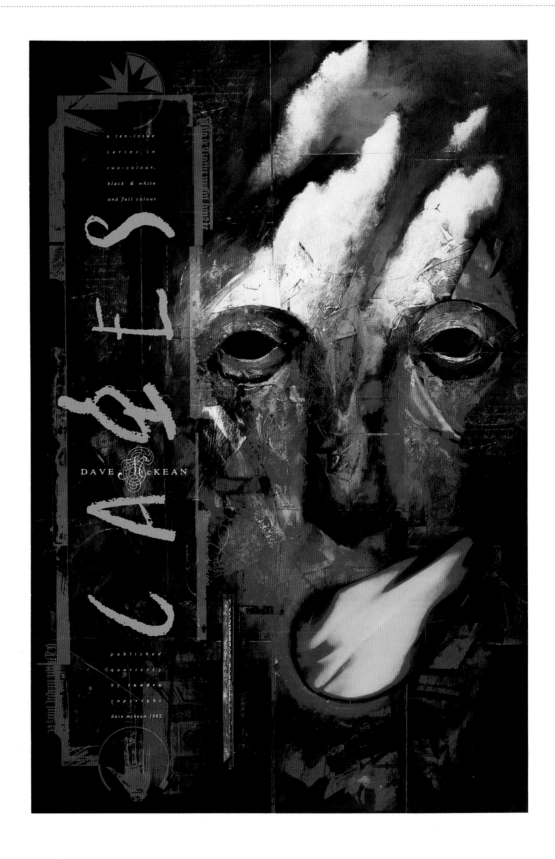

Volker Sträter

tel: **071 254 2856**   fax: **071 241 6049**

Agent: début art
52 Barbauld Road
London
N16 0SB

Title: Ananya

Medium: Collage & mixed media

Purpose of Work: Poster campaign to promote ananya products

Brief: To create a feminine, oriental and mysterious image to promote the perfume

Commissioned by: Collette McAlpin *The Body Shop*

Mike Trevithick

tel: **071 586 6032**

43 Upper Park Road
London
NW3 2UL

Medium: Clay acrylic, rice, pulses and beans

Purpose of Work: Poster

Brief: To create an image of a healthy family, using natural foods and All-Bran.

Commissioned by: Justin McCarthy, J.Walter Thompson

Client: Kelloggs All-Bran c/o JWT

50

Stephen Caplin

tel: **071 485 9290** fax: **071 267 9843**

117 Brecknock Road
London N19 5AE

Title: Stella Artois Tennis Tournament

Medium: Computer illustration from a photographic source

Purpose of Work:
To advertise Stella Artois Tennis Tounament

Commissioned by: Kevin Jones & Paul Hodginson *Lowe Howard Spink*

Photographer: Malcolm Venille

The Stella Artois. Queen's Club. June 7-13. Tickets: 071 497 0521.

The Stella Artois. Queen's Club. June 7-13. Tickets: 071 497 0521.

Peter Warner

tel: **0959 577270**

Boundary View
Hillside Road
Tatsfield
Kent
TN16 2NH

Title: Go-Cat

Medium: Watercolour

Purpose of Work: Packaging

Brief: To create a cat with the verve, energy, vitality and mischief implied by the petfood's brand name. It also had to be different in colour and breed to its competitors and is thus a cinnamon tabby, like my own cat

Commissioned by: Steve Elliot *Design Bridge*

Client: Nestlé

The print and design section was judged by:

Pamela Gowling
Head of Art - Rapier Steal & Bowden

Paul Rollo
Art Director - Decca Records

Alan Herron
Director - Giant

Geraldine Walsh
Production Manager - Brewer Riddiford

Ruairidh Lappin
R.L Associates - Design Consultants

winners

Book

Advertising

Print & Design

Information & Technology

Unpublished Student

Unpublished Professional

Newcomers

Michael Sheehy

tel: 081 693 4315 **fax: 081 693 4315**

115 Crystal Palace Road
East Dulwich
London
SE22 9ES

Title: 'Your paper, sir'

Medium: Mixed media

Brief: To provide a response to the given quote with reference to the achievements of WH Smith Ltd.

Commissioned by: Michael Heanue Design

54

Andrew Kingham

tel: **071 613 2323**   fax: **071 613 2726**

c/o The Inkshed
98 Columbia Road
London
E2 7QB

Title: Megacities: The Evil of Air Pollution

Medium: Metal

Purpose of Work: Annual report

Brief: To create a cover and two other illustrations
reflecting the College's environmental research worldwide

Commissioned by: Chiew Yong & John Rushworth *Pentagram Design Ltd.*

Client: King's College London

David Sim

tel: 031 667 8592   **fax: 031 662 4631**

5 Cobden Crescent
Edinburgh
EH9 2BG

Title: London

Medium: Watercolour &
coloured paper collage

Purpose of Work: Brochure cover

Brief: To produce an illustrated map of London
showing all the main points of interest for foreign students

Commissioned by: Andy Harrison *Harrison Radley*

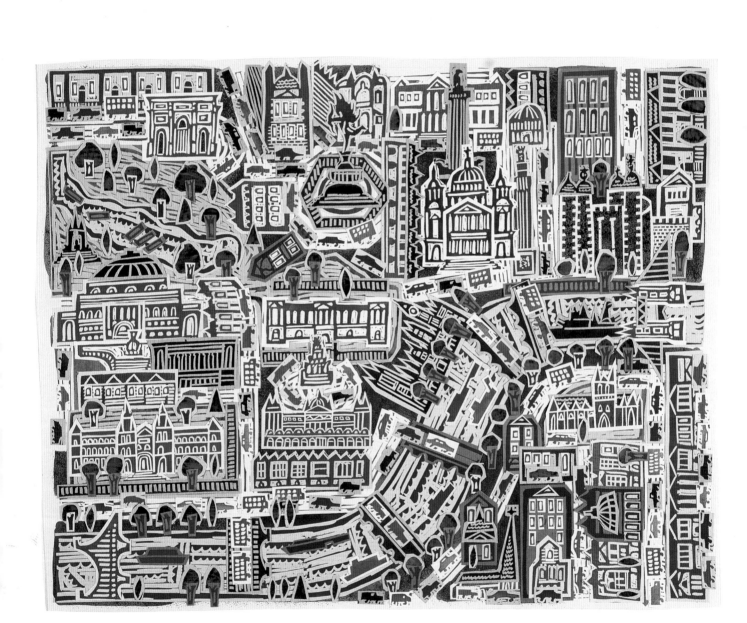

John Brennan

tel: **071 613 2323**   fax: **071 613 2726**

c/o **The Inkshed**
98 Columbia Road
London
E2 7QB

Title: Bigger Balls

Purpose of Work:
Agent's New Year promotional newspaper

Brief: To illustrate the notion that 1993 will see an enlargement in the size of footballs following claims that the present ball size makes the game too easy

Commissioned by: Jacqueline Hollister

Lara Harwood

tel: **071 739 7765**   fax: **071 613 2341**

c/o Big Orange
2nd Floor Back Building
150 Curtain Road
London
EC2A 3AR

92A Richmond Road
Kingston
Surrey KT2 5EN

tel: 081 549 9712

Title: Mango and Papya

Purpose of Work: Supermarket toiletry packaging

Brief: To produce a dynamic, colourful and distinctive illustration for a supermarket's new range of toiletries

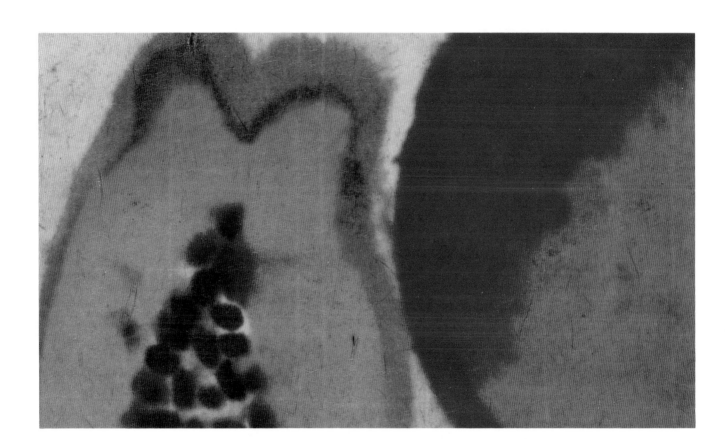

Liz Pichon

fax: 081 451 2521   tel: 081 451 0082

20 Harlesden Road
Willesden
London
NW10

Title: Gold Fish

Medium: Inks & acrylic

Purpose of Work:
Greetings card and wrapping paper

Brief: To design a motif which could
be repeated for general stationery purposes

Commissioned by: Simon Nevin *Canonbury Design*

David Faithfull

tel: **031 556 6063**

16 Park Road
Eskbank Dalkeith
Midlothian
EH22 3DH

Title: Festival of the Environment 1992

Medium: Recycled collage

Purpose of Work:
Poster and pamphlet cover to promote
the 1992 Festival of the Environment

Brief: To create an image employing recycled materials,
reflecting a "global" concept - the theme of that particular year's festival

Commissioned by: City of Edinburgh District Council

Client: The Department of Environmental Health in
collaboration with Smith Anderson Recycled Papers

Keren Ludlow

tel: **081 567 2653**

28 Hamilton Road
London
W5 2EH

Title: Sports Games Pastimes (Summer Collection 1993))

Medium: Lino print

Purpose of Work: Scarf and fabric design for summer clothes, brochure cover and T-shirts for fashion house

Brief: To create a sporty design with a traditional English feel to complement and focus the collection

Commissioned by: Ally Capellino

Ian Craig

tel: 081 291 1110   fax: 081 291 1557

c/o **Private View Artist's Agency**
26 Levendale Road
London
SE23 2TW

Title: Rossini String Sonatas

Medium: Photo collage

Purpose of Work: Compact disc cover

Brief: To create a bright, abstract image to convey the lively, joyous feel of the music

Commissioned by: Paul Rollo *The Decca Record Company Ltd.*

62

Fletcher Sibthorp

tel: **071 924 2473**

134 Salcott Road
London
SW11 6DG

Title: Jowett's Runners

Medium: Oil on canvas

Purpose of Work:
Cover for promotional brochure

Brief: To depict Jowetts Direct, a data to door mailing service, as the middle runner between the client and the Royal Mail and as a fast and highly-tuned connection between the two

Commissioned by: Cara *The Original Organisation*

Client: Jowetts Direct

Maggie Sawkins

tel: 071 359 0160

82 Highbury New Park
London
N5 2DJ

Title: Whirling Dervishes

Medium: Acrylic

Purpose of Work: Calendar illustration

Brief: To provide a positive and exciting image to represent Turkey

Commissioned by: Craig Methuen *Amnesty International*

64

Title: Whirling Dervishes

Medium: Acrylic

Purpose of Work: Calendar illustration

Brief: To provide a positive and exciting image to represent Turkey

Commissioned by: Craig Methuen *Amnesty International*

Ian Pollock

tel: **0625 426205**   fax: **0625 500617**

14 Crompton Road
Maccelsfield
Cheshire
SK11 8DS

Title: Interact

Medium: Watercolour, ink and gouche

Commisioned by: Nick Thirkell of Carroll, Dempsey & Thirkell Design Consultants for the W.H. Smith Arts Programme 1992-1993

David Loftus

tel: **071 381 9145**

31 Prothero Road
Fulham
London
SW6 7LY

Title: Pharmaceutical

Medium: Collage / gouache

Purpose of Work:
Corporate brochure cover

Brief: Cover needed to represent the pharmaceutical and research industry and to convey the company's international standing.

Commissioned by: Chico Ramos *Shaw Design*

Client: Inversek Research International Ltd.

66

The information and technology section was judged by:

David J Bradley
Civil Service illustrator

Amanda Evans
Freelance natural history illustrator

Jeffrey Brockwell
Freelance technical illustrator

Mustafa Sami
Commissioning Editor, technical and natural illustration

Neil Bulpitt
Freelance technical illustrator

winners

Book

Advertising

Print & Design

Information & Technology

Unpublished Student

Unpublished Professional

Professional

Newcomers

Jonathan Piers Tyler

tel: 0202 511763   fax: 0202 511763

12 Bingham Road
Bournemouth
Dorset
BH9 1BS

Title: Woodland Flowers of Spring

Purpose of Work: College course

Brief: To portray wildflowers in their natural surroundings, taking composition, light and botanical accuracy into account, to raise awareness of the plight of some of our rarer wildflowers

Hayley Simmons

tel: **0722 412227**   fax: **0722 414179**

7A Catherine Street
Salisbury
Wiltshire
SP1 2DF

Medium: Watercolour & gouache

Purpose of Work: College project

I work mainly in watercolour and gouache, sometimes incorporating a little airbrushing. I have a special interest in book illustration and will be pursuing this in the future

Philip Hockey

tel: 0202 533011   fax: 0202 537729

c/o Bournemouth & Poole
College of Art & Design
Wallisdown Road
Poole
Dorset BH12 5HH

Title: H.M.S. Gannet 1878,
shown as refitted in 1886

Purpose of Work: Illustration to be
permanently displayed alongside the ship
and to be reproduced as a poster for sale
to the public in support of the restoration

Brief: To show how the ship was in 1886 in the most
accurate and visually interesting way as possible

Commissioned by: Maritime Trust London

HMS GANNET 1878

Don Nother

tel: **0202 533011**   fax: **0202 537729**

c/o **Bournemouth & Poole**
College of Art & Design
Wallisdown Road
Poole
Dorset BH12 5HH

Title: Steam Tug 'Portwey' 1927

Purpose of work:
Poster and Christmas card

Brief: To promote the ongoing
restoration and running of the tug

Commissioned by: The Maritime Trust

THE STEAM TUG *PORTWEY* 1927

Drawn by Don Nother 1992
The School of Illustration
Bournemouth and Poole College of Art and Design

Leighton Moses

tel: 0443 740522

2 Well Street
Carnetown
Abercynon
Mid. Glamorgan CF45 4PT
South Wales

Title: Common Buzzard

Medium: Acrylic

Purpose of Work: College Project

Brief: To depict a bird of prey in its habitat, in this case a common buzzard on the Gilfach Rhydd Mountain, Mid. Glamorgan

Leighton Moses

tel: **0443 740522**

2 Well Street
Carnetown
Abercynon
Mid. Glamorgan CF45 4PT
South Wales

Title: A Cross Section of the River Stour

Medium: Acrylic

Purpose of Work:
Poster for a commercial project

Brief: To highlight the natural history of the River Stour

Commissioned by: Bournemouth Parks and Recreation Dept.

David Penney

tel: 081 341 0529

49A Langdon Park Road
Highgate
London N6 5PT

Title: Marine Timekeeping stamps

Medium: Watercolour

Purpose of Work: Series of stamps commemorating the pioneering work of John Harrison

Brief: To produce four views of Harrison's prizewinning timekeeper H4, showing view of pierced and engraved movement

Commissioned by: Howard Brown

Client: Royal Mail

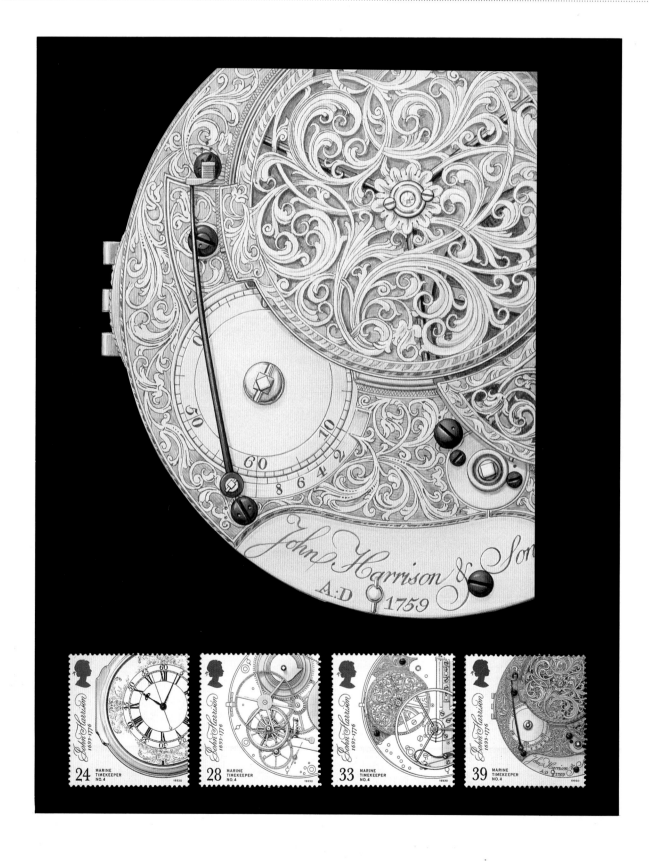

The unpublished student section was judged by:

Sarah Ball
Illustrator

Deborrah George
Art Director - New Scientist

Ian Pape
Design Director - Thumb Design

Stuart Thomas
Art Director - Just 17 Magazine

Shaun Westgate
Uffindale and West

winners

Book

Advertising

Print & Design

Information & Technology

Unpublished Student

Unpublished Professional

Newcomers

Jeremy Roberts

tel: **0554 752387**

19A Stradley Hill
Pwll
Llanelli
Dyfed
SA15 4AB

Title: Easy Money?

Medium: Acrylic

Purpose of Work: Final college project

Brief: To accompany an article on the subject of banks lending money and what happens to you, the target, when things get out of hand

76

Frazer Lyndon Hudson

tel: **071 328 8100**

34 Priory Terrace
West Hampstead
London
NW6 4DH

Title: Pantomime Horse
Performance / Life's a Pantomime

Medium: Pen & ink wash photocopied on Xerox 5775

Purpose of Work: Self-initiated, to be used eventually as a book cover

Brief: A series of black & white illustrations emphasising a book of proverbs

Martin Port

tel: **0635 868127**

3 Sagecroft Road
Thatcham
Berkshire
RG13 4BU

Title: Amnesty International Calendar

Medium: 3-D mixed media

Purpose of Work: Illustration for a calendar

Brief: To show the motivation behind the cause

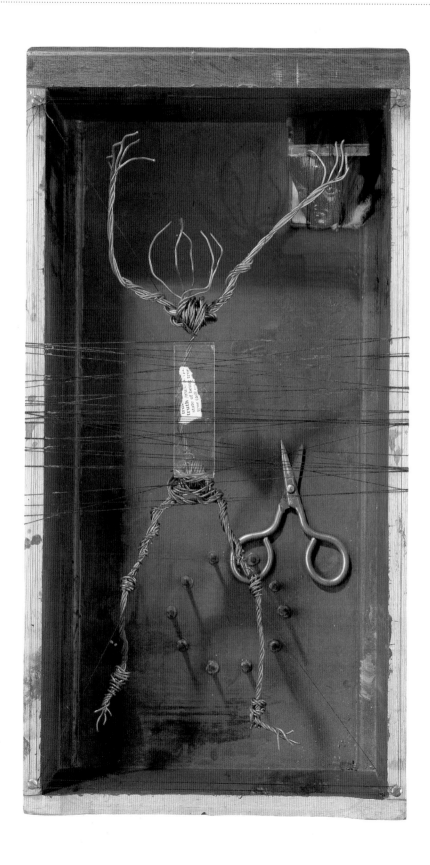

Nick Patrick

4 Down Lane
Frant
Tunbridge Wells
Kent TN3 9HW

Title: The Midnight Meat Train

Medium: Acrylic & Conte pastels

Purpose of Work: Final college project

Brief: To create a book jacket for this short story and imbue it with a gritty realism

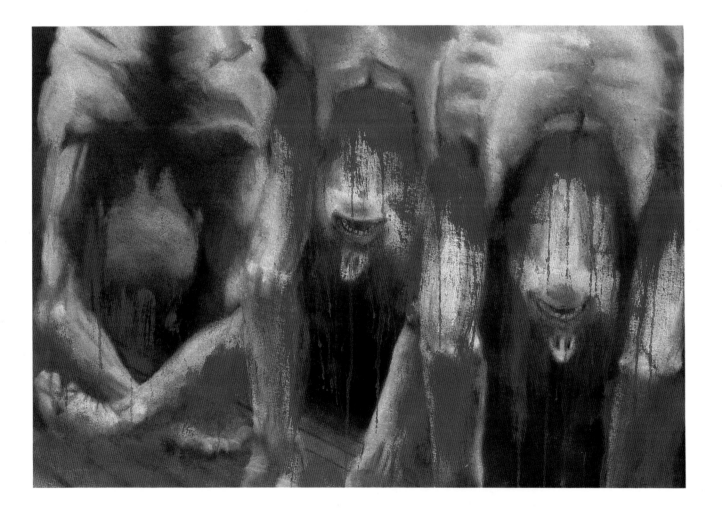

Elena Gomez

tel: **081 861 2975 / 0483 414786**

62 Toorack Road
Harrow Weald
Middlesex
HA3 5HU

Title: La Mancha

Medium: Painted collage

Purpose of Work:
Wine label for college major project

Brief: This is one of a set of ten wine labels
from around the world.
This one is La Mancha in Central Spain

Daniel Mackie

tel: **081 650 5260**

75 Cedars Road
Beckenham
Kent
BR3 4JQ

Title: The Wasp Factory

Medium: Acrylic & ink modified
with computer techniques

Purpose of Work: Students project

Brief: To design a display card
and jacket for launch of new book

Robert Pittam

tel: **0788 544228**

75 Wentworth Road
Rugby
Warwickshire
CV22 6BQ

Title: Seen and Not Seen

Purpose of Work: College project

Brief: To illustrate a short story about a misfit who believed that by concentrating on the of an ideal he would assume that character's appearance and potency

82

Brad Gray

tel: **0291 624878**

5 Danes Hill
Sedbury
Chepstow
Gwent
NP6 7BA

1: Title: Male Prostitution

Medium: Oil, alkyd, acrylic, biro & masking tape

Purpose of Work: Editorial

Brief: To illustrate a piece depicting the mood and feelings to do with male prostitution

2: Title: Patience   **Purpose of Work:** Editorial

Medium: Acrylic, oil, alkyd & biro

Brief: To accompany an article about the virtues. I chose patience, which to me is best represented by queueing

3: Title: The Diceman

Medium: Oil & alkyd

Purpose of Work: Bookjacket

Brief: To create a bold and striking image for The Diceman by Luke Rhinehart

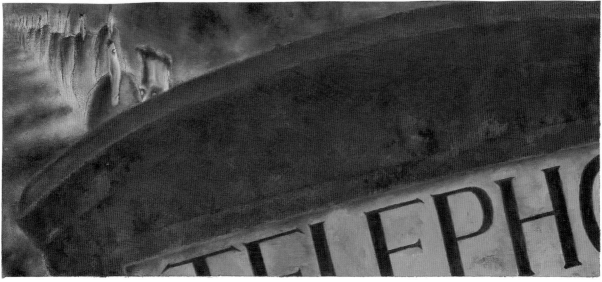

Jill S. Calder

tel: **031 226 5754**

Studio Six
Castle Cliff Workshops
25 Johnstone Terrace
Edinburgh

Title: Facial Disfigurement

Medium: Ink & chalk pastels

Purpose of Work: Personal

Brief: A drawing depicting street-life in Barcelona

84

The unpublished professional section was judged by:

Stuart Briers
Illustrator

Helen Surman
Senior Designer - Penguin / Puffin

Tim Foster
Art Director - Reed Books

John Tenant
Creative Director - Woman's Journal

Sue McNally
Senior Designer - Times Saturday Reveiw

winners

Book

Advertising

Print & Design

Information & Technology

Unpublished Student

Unpublished Professional

Professional

Newcomers

Martin Cooper

tel: **081 595 3388**   fax: **081 595 3388**

37 Stanley Avenue
Dagenham
Essex
RM8 1JH

Agency:
Artbank International

tel: 081 906 2288
fax: 081 906 2289

Title: Ball & Chain

Medium: Acrylic on canvas

Purpose of Work: Self-promotional

Brief: To illustrate an article about boredom at work and the slow trudge of time

Martin Cooper

tel: **081 595 3388**   fax: **081 595 3388**

37 Stanley Avenue
Dagenham
Essex
RM8 1JH

Agency:
Artbank International

tel: 081 906 2288
fax: 081 906 2289

Title: The Abacus

Medium: Acrylic on canvas

Purpose of Work: Self-promotional

Brief: To produce an illustration to accompany an article
'Computers Past and Present', showing some stage of computer history

Patrick MacAllister

15 Lauderdale House
Gosling Way
London SW9 6JS

tel: 071 582 3344

Title: Designed for a Clockface

Medium: Gouache

Brief: Self-promotional

MAGNET

88

Carolyn Gowdy

tel: 071 731 5380

2C Maynard Close
(off Cambria Street)
London
SW6 2EN

Title: Heart in Danger

Medium: Mixed

Purpose of Work
Part of a one-woman exhibition entitled Human Comedies

Satoshi Kambayashi

tel: **0273 771539**   fax: **0273 771539**

79 Payne Avenue
Hove
East Sussex
BN3 5HD

Agent
Ian Fleming

tel: **071 734 8701**
fax: **071 439 3400**

Title: Minema

Medium: India ink & watercolour

Purpose of Work: Self-promotion

Brief: To characterise Minema movie theatre in Knightsbridge, London after the caption in the brochure - 'a tiny cinema for exclusive tastes' - and personal experience

Paul Campion

tel: **0202 317014**   fax: **0202 317014**

Room C2
Ellerslie Chambers
2 Hinton Road
Bournemouth
Dorset BH1 2EF

Agent: Folio

tel: 071 242 9562
fax: 071 242 1816

Title: A Visit to the Mother-in-law

Medium: Acrylic

Purpose of Work:
Self-promotional

Brief: To produce a fantasy/horror piece experimenting with distorted forced perspective and to create a horrific, squeamish-looking monster.

Greg Becker

tel: **081 693 6120**   fax: **081 693 6120**

41 Whately Road
East Dulwich
London
SE22 9DE

Title: Princess Caraboo
from the Island of Jevasu

Medium: Watercolour

Brief: Inspired by The English Eccentrics by Edith Sitwell

Lisa Berkshire

tel: 0904 652515

The Fishergate Centre
4 Fishergate
York
YO1 4AB

Title: A Good October

Medium: Acrylic

Purpose of Work: Calendar

Brief: To depict the proverb:
A good October and a good blast
To blow the acorn and the mast

Madeleine Smith

tel: **0296 21536**   fax: **0296 21536**

13 Grasmere
Bedgrove Park
Aylesbury
HP21 9TU

Medium: Acrylic

Purpose of Works: Personal project

Brief: To depict the domination of people by the man-made environment

Bill Butcher

tel: **071 729 9184**   fax: **071 739 9558**

43 Coronet Street
London
N1 6HD

Title: Social Violence

Brief: To depict a potentially dangerous
situation and portray how you could deal with it

Client: Sunday Times Magazine

Stuart Briers

tel: **081 767 2618**   fax: **081 767 2618**

33 Eswyn Road
London
SW17 8TR

Title: Harmony

Brief: A visual interpretation
of the word 'harmony'

MAGNET

Stuart Briers

tel: **081 767 2618**   fax: **081 767 2618**

33 Eswyn Road
London
SW17 8TR

Title: Changed to a Cat

Purpose of Work: Experimental

David Smith

tel: 0737 814189   fax: 0737 814190

65 Breech Lane
Walton on the Hill
Tadworth
Surrey
KT20 7SJ

Title: Totem Automatika

Medium: Mixed-media

Purpose of Work: Self-promotional

Brief: To capture the feelings of anxiety associated with a technological age

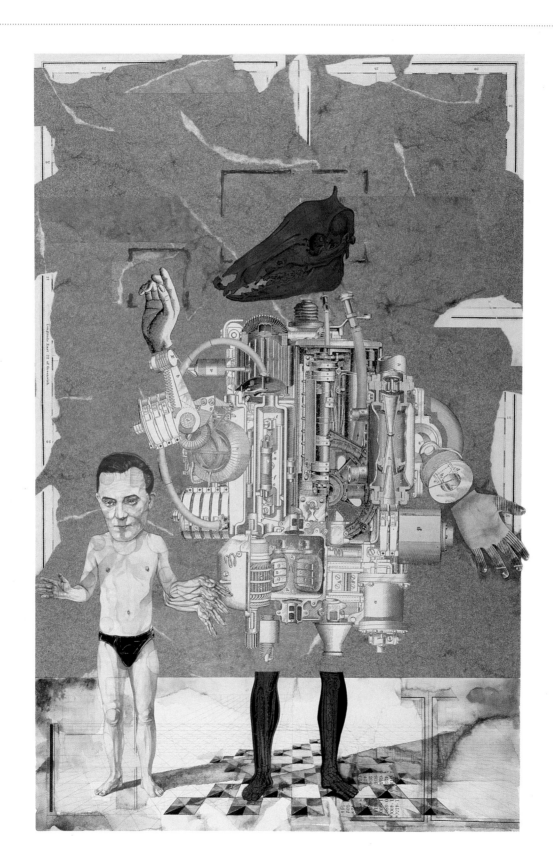

Gale Pitt

tel: **081 989 7265**   fax: **081 989 7265**

32 Felstead Road
Wanstead
London
E11 2QJ

Title: State Circus

Medium: Oil

Purpose of Work: Fun

I have illustrated childrens' books and developed fantasy paintings which sell in Japan.

I design decorative tin boxes for *International Can* in Hong Kong and will tackle any subject in oil or watercolour

Georgios Manoli

tel: 081 597 2457   fax: 081 597 2457

397 Whalebone Lane North
Chadwell Heath
Romford
Essex RM6 6RH

Agent: Artbank International
8 Woodcroft Avenue
London NW7 2AG

tel: 081 906 2288
fax: 081 906 2289

Title: Three Cup Trick

Medium: Acrylic on canvas

Brief: The gamble of small businesses venturing onto the European market

Georgios Manoli

tel: **081 597 2457**   fax: **081 597 2457**

397 Whalebone Lane North
Chadwell Heath
Romford
Essex RM6 6RH

Agent: Artbank International
8 Woodcroft Avenue
London NW7 2AG

tel: 081 906 2288
fax: 081 906 2289

Title: The Smoker

Medium: Acrylic on canvas

Brief: Cutting the habit with the use of hypnosis

Len Shelley

tel: **0424 437828**

8 Courtlands Flats
West Hill Road
St. Leonards-on-sea
Hastings
East Sussex TN38 0NA

Title: The Butcher's Fear of the Carcase

Medium: Multi-media box construction

Purpose of Work: Personal project

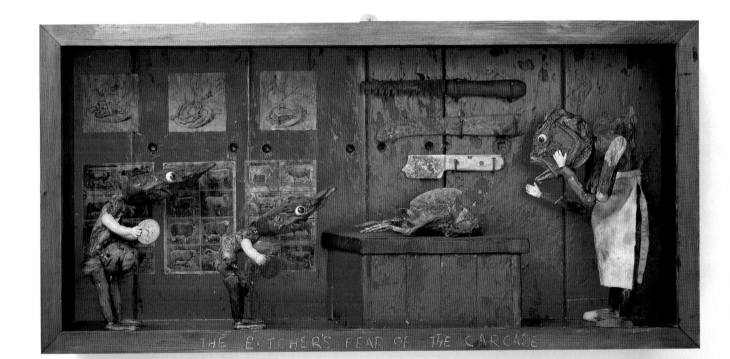

Geoffrey Appleton

tel: **0538 300401**

New York Farm
near Upper Elkstone
One Cote
Leek
Staffs

Title: Chris and June

Medium: Acrylic

Purpose of Work: Self-promotional

Geoffrey Appleton

tel: 0538 300401

New York Farm
near Upper Elkstone
One Cote
Leek
Staffs

Title: Streatham

Medium: Acrylic

Purpose of Work: Self-promotional

Brief: An on-going project of a series of illustrations called 'The Victoria Line'

104

Geoffrey Appleton

tel: **0538 300401**

New York Farm
near Upper Elkstone
One Cote
Leek
Staffs

Title: Brixton

Medium: Acrylic

Purpose of Work: Self-promotional

Brief: An on-going project of a series of illustrations called 'The Victoria Line'

Bill Sanderson

tel: **0480 461506**

Fernleigh
Huntingdon Road
Houghton
Cambs. PE17 2AU

Title: Bristol Centre 1790

Medium: Scraperboard

Purpose of Work: Book illustration

Brief: To illustrate *Treasure Island* by Robert Louis Stephenson by depicting Bristol City Centre Docks in 1790

Ian Pollock

fax: **0625 500617**   tel: **0625 426205**

14 Crompton Road
Maccelsfield
Cheshire
SK11 8DS

Title: Watchful Servants

Medium: Watercolour, ink and gouache

Purpose of work: Personal project entitled 'The Parables of Christ'. Watchful servants (Luke 12 : 35-40) — For the son of man is coming at an hour you do not expect

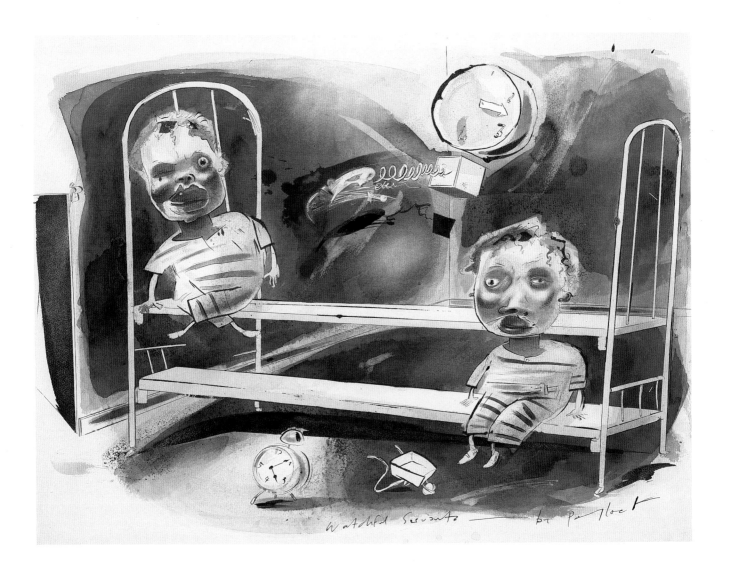

part 2

Book

Advertising

Print & Design

Information & Technology

Unpublished Student

Unpublished Professional

Professional

Newcomers

Jonny Mendelsson

tel: 081 455 0168   fax: 081 455 0168

57 Leeside Crescent
London
NW11 0HA

Title: On The Road: New York

Medium: 3-D montage

Purpose of Work: Editorial series

Commissioned by: Chris Krage *The Times Saturday Review*

I work exclusively in montage, flat & in relief

Clients include: Ayer, Howell Henry, Greys, TheTimes, The Observer, The Body Shop, Radio Times, Creative Magazines, Berkeley Magazines, Cassel & Vintage, Redwood, EMAP and IPC

Michael Jackson

tel: **081 671 0085**   fax: **081 671 0085**

28 Tenham Avenue
London
SW2 4XR

Title (1): Wanking Affects Your Eyesight

Medium: Screen print

Purpose of Work: Personal project

Title (2): Impecunious Fiddler

Medium: Screen print

Purpose of Work: Personal project

Tracey Hayden

tel: **071 351 1246**

2 Crofton House
32 Old Church Street
London
SW3 5BZ

My main interest is architecture but other subjects include food, flora and travel

I work with various media, mixing acrylic paint, coloured pencil and oil pastel. Main areas of work include publishing, editorial, greetings cards and postcards

The work below shows Piccadilly Circus at night and The Royal Albert Hall. Both images have been used for postcards

Peter Gudynas — *Zap Art*

tel: **021 459 0080**   fax: **021 459 0080**

89 Hazlewell Crescent
Stirchley
Birmingham
B30 2QE

The use of digital psycho-graphic-technodelic media to explore a new type of techno-surrealism - the posthuman image modified and synthesised by certain applications of science and technology, mediated by post modernist science fiction / fact speculation > Speculative Illustrations: the imagery of anthropomorphic machines, human machine interfaces, artificially intelligent sentient beings, virtual reality cyberspace simulations, cyberpunk technoir scenarios, set in hypothetical futures not so far removed from our own present   > Fact or Fiction? < Zero Time

Angela Dundee

tel: **041 334 4403**

c/o S. Scotland
6 Woodlands Drive
Glasgow
G4 9EH

Agent Paris:
Maureen Sale

tel: **010 331 42 24 09 67**

Medium: Cut paper & Conte pastel

Purpose of Work: Editorial

Brief: To accompany articles about
Easter ski-ing holidays in Europe

Commissioned by: David Curless *The Times Saturday Review*

Vikki Liogier

tel: 081 682 0780   **fax: 081 682 0780**

12 Brenda Road
entrance in Mandrake Road
London
SW17 7DB

MAGNET

Title: Banking in Europe / Development in Banking Technology

Purpose of Work: Magazine cover

Commissioned by: Nathalie Williams
Harrington Kilbride PLC

Clients include: Diners Club International, IBM, Gordons Gin, TWA, Boots, DMB & B, Paperchase, WH Smith, Safeway, Radio Times, Mail on Sunday, Gemplus International, Robinson Club (Germany), MC Cann Direct, Groupe Steelcase Strafor, M6 (French TV), Vogue, Marie-Claire, Penguin Books, Bloomsbury and Heinemann International.
See Images 17 & Contact 7, 8 & 9

Henning Löhlein

tel: **0272 532879**

14 Glathorne Road
Southville
Bristol
BS3 1LU

Title: Dreams Come True

Medium: Acrylic

Purpose of Work: Magazine article

Brief: Buying surplus computer equipment can be a great way of securing great bargains.

Commissioned by: John Gash *PC Direct*

Clients include: The Observer Magazine, Design Week, Dennis Publishing, EMAP and Macmillan Publishing

Jon Hamilton

tel: **071 254 2856**   fax: **071 241 6049**

Agent:

début art
52 Barbauld Road
London N16 OST

1: Purpose of Work:
Self-promotional brochure

Commissioned by: Torch Associates

2: Commissioned by:
RM Associates Film Distributors

Previous clients include:
IBM, British Telecom, Mercury, ICI, Ford, Digital, Scottish Hydro Electric, Barclays Bank, The Henley Forecasting Centre, Central TV, Decca Record Company, Sappi Graphics, Harper Collins Publishing, MacUser Magazine, Banking Technology and More Magazine

Susie Louis

tel: **081 749 2885**

Computer programmes I mainly work in are: Nimbus,Drawmouse, Amiga - Duluxe Paint,
Apple Macintosh - Photoshop & P.C. Corel Draw
I create images for company logos, publishing, brochures and record covers

Clients include: English Tourist Board, World Runners, Nim Nim Musik, City Bank, Bella, GE Publishing and Arista Records

118

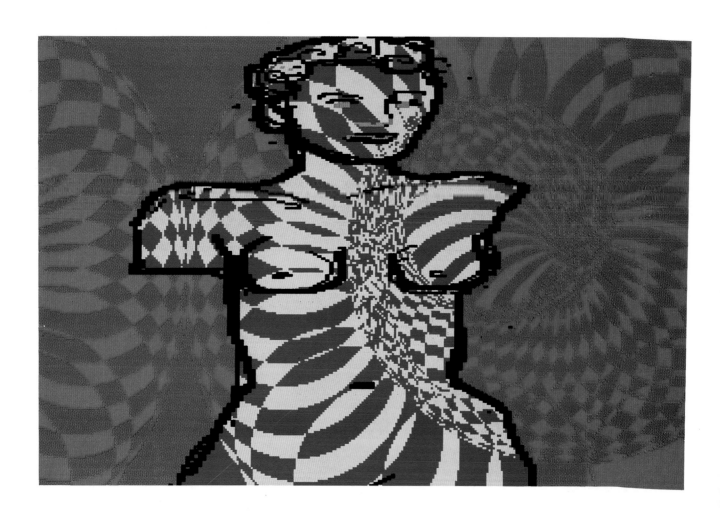

Paul Burgess

tel: **081 852 1600**   fax: **081 852 1600**

73 Pascoe Road
London
SE13 5JE

Medium:
Collage / 3-D Mixed-media illustration

Purpose of Work:
Pepe promotional poster / Pepe Art Series
Printed as poster & magazine

Brief: To produce an illustration using
images from recent Pepe fashion shoots

Commissioned by: Leigh Marling *Blue Source Design*

Andrew Fowler

tel: **0734 267800**   fax: **0734 267800**

593 London Road
Earley
Reading
Berkshire
RG6 1AT

Title: Pineapple Fish

Medium: Lino cut on Japanese straw paper

Purpose of Work:
To illustrate a recipe on Hawaiian cooking

Max Ellis

Max Ellis

tel: **081 995 4771**   fax: **081 995 4771**

22 Thorney Hedge Road
London
W4 5SD

Title: Dancing Partners

Medium: Acrylic

Purpose of Work: Magazine illustration

Commissioned by:
Paul Bowden *GQ Magazine*

Brief: To depict the special relationship between David English, Editor of the Daily Mail, and John Major. The illustration is based on an adaptation of the adage *'being in someone's pocket'*

Max Ellis has been working as an illustrator since 1986, winning the AOI Award for the Best Use of Humour in 1992. He contributes regularly to the Radio Times, Redwood Publishing, Reed Business Publishing, Dennis Publishing, HHL Publishing and various advertising agencies, record companies and book publishers

121

Tristram Woolston

tel: **071 734 8671**   fax: **071 434 1808**
mobile: **0374 490898**

7-11 Lexington Street
London
W1R 4BU

Tristram specialises in the illustration of buildings and places - architectural, industrial and landscape

He works in watercolour or line and wash, using on-the-spot sketches, architects plans or photographic reference

Recent commissions range from brochure illustrations of chemical plants and industrial processes for Associated Octel to the visualisation of a new consular building for the Foreign & Commonwealth Office in Islamabad

The drawing is from a series of London shops, restaurants and wine bars

Jolyne Knox

tel: 081 852 9602

33 The Plantation
London
SE3 0AB

Media: Watercolour, ink &
pencil.line & scraperboard

My main interest is book illustration, having produced over one hundred books, mainly for children. Selected titles have been chosen for the Smarties Prize list in Great Britain and as Children's Book of the Year by the USA Children's Book Committee. I specialize in figurative and imaginative work and welcome the opportunity to visually develop character and ideas

I also undertake natural history illustration which complements other work

Mary Stubberfield c/o AOI

tel: **071 631 1510**

Agent:
The London Art Collection

tel: 071 376 7773
fax: 071 376 7576

Title: Utopia

Medium: Inks, bleach & marbled paper

Purpose of Work:
Self-motivated experiment

I also work in black & white lino prints

Recent clients include:
Victor Gollancz, Womens' Press, Goldwell's Hair
Products, Co-Op Supermarket, Redwood Publishing & Radio Times

Sarah Perkins

studio tel: **071 357 6114**   fax: **071 357 6442**

37E Guiness Court
Snowfields
London SE1 3SX

tel: 071 378 1510

Studio:
McArthur / Fry Studio
54-58 Tanner Street
London SE1

Agent: The Inkshed
98 Columbia Road
London E2 7QB

tel: 071 613 2323
fax: 071 613 2726

1: Title: Coffee with a Conscience

Commissioned by: Country Living

2: Title Body & Soul

Commissioned by: Options

Clients include: Penguin, Virago, Random Century, Andre Deutsch, Victor Gollancz, Elle, Marie Claire, New Scientist, New Statesman, The Observer, The Independent, The Guardian, EMI, Scottish National Ballet, Ernst and Young, Shell and Vauxhall Motors

Simon Shaw

tel: **031 225 8235**

45 (1F2) Well Court
Dean Village
Edinburgh

Title (1): Open Road

Medium: Acrylic & watercolour on paper

Purpose of Work
To illustrate Zen and the Art
of Motorcycle Maitenance

(2): Untitled

Medium: Pen & ink
Based on part of Aberdeen Library

Commissioned by: Network Magazine

Please call if you would like to see more

Mark Dobson

tel: **081 689 1427**   fax: **081 689 1427**

c/o Steven Wells
Illustration Agency
PO Box 651
London SE25 5PS

Purpose of Work:
To accompany an article
entitled *Never Never Land*

Brief: To depict property owners
who cannot control their payments

Commissioned by: Charlotte Hollis *Reed Publishing*

David Parkinson

tel: **0932 857947**   fax: **0932 857947**

8 Western Hay
High Pine Close
Weybridge
Surrey
KT13 9EA

Title: Between A.R. and E.H.

Medium: Conte pencils

Purpose of Work: Book jacket

Commissioned by: Grafix Montreal Quebec

Brief: To illustrate a photo-montage on Ooralism.
The title stands for A Trans-Atlantic Rehabilitation
of Pataphysics in Post-Stucturalist-Phenomenological Form

This involvement fits my more normal style of mixed / multi-media canned-chance assemblages / ensembles - found (as in Marcel Duchamp) in any mode or zone of human behaviour and communication

Michael Bramman

tel: **071 723 3564**

104 Dudley Court
Upper Berkeley Street
London
W1H 7PJ

Title: Jerry

Barbara Loftus

tel: **0273 736310**

56 Brunswick Square
Hove
East Sussex
BN3 1EF

Title: Arts Sponsorship

Medium: Acrylic

Purpose of Work: Feature in *Address*
(The Royal Mail Magazine for Business)

Commissioned by: Laurie Caddell

P.M. Chappell

Studio tel: 071 436 4146   **fax: 071 580 8979**

44 Beechwood Close
Little Chalfont
Bucks HP6 6QX

tel: 0494 762484

Clients include: The Milk Marketing Board, Linguaphone, Europe Assistance, Cambridge University Press & The Lyric Theatre.

I also work in black & white

Sue Cony

tel: 0799 541439

2 Patmore Cottages
High Street
Debden
Saffron Walden
Essex CB11 3LF

Clients include: BBC Playdays, Camden
Graphics, Ginn, Walker, Two-can, Heinemann,
Joshua Morris, Scholastic, OUP, Marshall
Editions, World International, Elsevier, Girl Guides
Association, Collins and Hodder & Stoughton

Satoshi Kambayashi

tel: **0273 771539**   fax: **0273 771539**

79 Payne Avenue
Hove
East Sussex
BN3 5HD

Agent: Ian Fleming

tel: **071 734 8701**
fax: **071 439 3400**

Graphic humorist specializing in humorous and conceptual illustration

Clients include: The International Herald Tribune, BBC Homes & Antiques, The Cartoonist, Heinemann International, Serpent's Tail, The In-House Lawyer, Punch, Die Welt, Horzu, Insight Japan and The Saturday Evening Post.

See also Images 17 & Art 93, 94.

John Eastwood

tel: **0273 843847** fax: **0273 843847**

6 Church Lane
Ditchling
Sussex
BN6 8TB

Medium: Mixed media & collage

Purpose of Work:
Self-promotional experiment

Brief: To design a book cover for The Selected Poetry of Rainer Maria Rilke and to evoke the strange, ethereal atmosphere of her poetry

134

Ian Hainsworth

tel: **0602 243596** fax: **0602 243596**

22 Ashfield Road
Nottingham
NG2 4LS

1: Medium: Gouache

Brief: To illustrate an article promoting the resurgence of hair pieces in fashion.

Commissioned by:
Jason Schulman *Tatler*

2: Medium: Mixed media

Purpose of Work:
To accompany magazine article Spirit of France

Commissioned by: Neil Watkinson
Sunday Observer Magazine

Philip Argent

tel: 071 267 8677

1 Lupton Street
London
NW5 2JA

Brief: Illustrations for cover and inside
The Times Saturday Review to accompany article
'The Case Against Therapy' by Fay Weldon

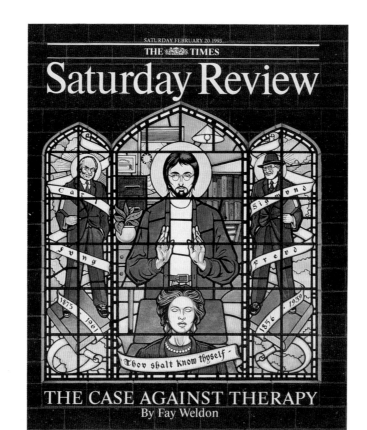

Samantha Pearce

tel: **0204 76703**

10 Exeter Avenue
Farnworth
Bolton
Greater Manchester
BL4 0NE

Title:1 Communication barriers

Title:2 Aquarius

After graduating in Graphic Design at University College, Salford, I have exhibited in various galleries within Manchester and recently finished a course in illustration at St. Martins School of Art in London

I illustrate for editorial, publishing, design and advertising

Kessia Beverley-Smith

tel: **0425 473125**   fax: **0425 473125**

Ravenscroft
Hurn Road
Ashley Ringwood
Hampshire
BH24 2AL

Title: Indian Montage

Medium: French polish &
acrylic over a paper relief

Purpose of Work: Experiment for portfolio

Brief: To create an interesting image in one colour

I have expanded into illustration on the Macintosh and won
a competition to design an advert for Canon in the August edition
of Creative Review, where the entire image was achieved on the computer

Kevin O'Brien

tel: **081 533 0614**   fax: **081 533 0614**

42 Newick Road
London
E5 0RR

Agent:
The Organisation

tel: 071 833 8268
     071 833 4161

Title: 5-Year Guarantee

Purpose of Work: One of several images in promotional brochure

Commissioned by: Jeff Pacione *Fitch RS*

Client; SVOBODA Scandinavian Furnishing Group

Mood, colour, tone, simplicity

Kevin has worked for a broad range of clients through major ad agencies, design groups and publishers, in the UK and abroad

Alan McGowan

tel: **031 552 5788**

37A Inverleith Row
Edinburgh

Represented outside Scotland by
The Organisation:
Jane Buxton   tel: 071 278 5176
Lorraine Owen   tel: 071 833 8268

140

Paul Hess

33B Kathleen Road
Lavender Hill
London
SW11 2JR

Agent: Garden Studio
23 Ganton Street
London W1V 1LA

tel: 071 287 9191

Peter Ingram

tel: **0992 717580**   fax: **0992 717580**

40 Queens Road
Waltham Cross
Herts
EN8 7HT

Left: InterCity 100

Top right: Self-promotion

Bottom right: Self-promotion

I have an extensive range of skills from the advertising industry. Specialities include airbrush, mixed-media illustration, line, wash and scraperboard

Areas of work include the video industry, brochures, print, packing, TV, the national press and Sunday supplements. I am interested in branching out into new fields of work

Video on request

Michaela Blunden

tel: **0273 770957**   fax: **0273 621005**

First floor flat
16 Norfolk Road
Brighton
East Sussex
BN1 3AA

1: Medium: Water collage

Purpose of Work: Book jacket for collection of African poetry entitled Napolo and the Python

Commissioned by: Heinemann

2: Title: The Weighing of the Worlds

Medium: Water collage

Purpose of Work: Book jacket for *The Power of Magic*

Commissioned by: Mitchell Beazley

Recent clients include:
Sainsburys, Westminster Borough Council, Company Magazine, Longmans, Radio Times, Namara Press, The Guardian, Hodder & Stoughton and Cambridge University Press

Lyn O'Neill

tel: **081 874 1712**   fax: **081 874 1712**

24 Longfield Street
London
SW18 5RE

1: Title: Wind - Power

2: Title: Getting Money For GP
Fundholders

Commissioned by: GP Magazine

3: Title: A Labour of Moles

Purpose of Work: Book illustration

Commissioned by:
Esmonde Publishing for their book of
collective nouns, A Crash of Rhinos

Recent clients include: Aries Design, EMAP Metro,
Butcher & Gunderson, Cadogan Books, Bauer Verlag,
Friends of the Earth, G.E. Publishing, Hammond Gower
Publications, IPC, National Magazines, OUP, Price
Waterhouse, Redwood Publishing, Safeways, Thomas
Nelson, Marks & Spencers, WH Smith, Womens' Press,
Ware Antony Rust, Wine Society and Harper Collins

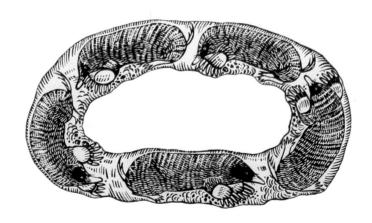

Neil Hague

tel: **081 543 2217**   fax: **081 543 1543**

176A Merton High Street
Wimbledon
London
SW19 1AY

Title: Seasons and Festivals

Medium: Gouache

Brief: To base the subject on both ancient and modern celebrations of time

Recent clients include: The Oxford University Press, BBC, Heinemann Educational, VNU Publications, Car Magazine, Centaur Communications, Thomas Nelson & Sons, Redwood Publishing, COI and The Economist

Please ring for a portfolio presentation.
See also Images 17 p.124

Tim Stevens

tel: 081 508 1974

40 Upper Park
Loughton
Essex
IG10 4EQ

Medium: Pen & ink and watercolour

Purpose of Work: Self-promotional book illustration, from *The Owl and the Pussycat*

My particular interests are in childrens' books and traditional British pen & ink work

Nancy Anderson

tel: 081 681 0310   **fax: 081 681 0310**

8A Birdhurst Rise
South Croydon
Surrey
CR2 7ED

Title: Computer Prospectus

Medium: Lino-cut & watercolour

Purpose of Work: Brochure cover

Commissioned by: Rob Silk
Tattersall, Hammerling & Silk

Client: Trinity Insurance Company Ltd.

MAGNET

Andrew Bylo

tel: **071 274 4116**   fax: **071 738 3743**

38B Southwell Road
London
SE5 9PG

Represented in France by:
Claire Prébois

tel: 010 331 46 24 12 22
fax: 010 331 46 40 72 51

Title: Niki Lauda

Commissioned by: Steve Devane

Client: Director

MAGNET

Neale Osborne

tel: **021 433 4729**

24 High Meadow Road
Kings Norton
Birmingham
B38 9AR

1: Title: Boardroom, Queen Elizabeth Hospital

2: Title: John Smith

3: Title: The Author, Russell Hoban

Recent work includes: Wisden Cricket Monthly, Warwickshire County Cricket Club, South Birmingham Health Authority, The Nursing Times, The Birmingham Post, Frontline, The Round Table Association and Mojo, the Rock & Roll Magazine.

Jean Ann O'Neill

tel: **0205 310522**

17 Princess Ann Road
Boston
Lincolnshire
PE21 9AP

1: Title: Modelling

Medium: Coloured pencil

Purpose of Work: Book

Commissioned by: Quarto Publishing

2: Title: Dolphins

Medium: Neocolour
Aquarelle / Coloured pencil

Purpose of Work:
Self-promotional for a greetings card

I work in a conventional semi-realistic style using coloured pencils and in a decorative style and design with Neocolour Aquarelle and coloured pencil

Jonathan Gill

tel: **071 733 9897**

209A Coldharbour Lane
London
SW9 8RU

1: Title: Stacy and the Mystery of Stoneybrook

2: Title: Jessi's Babysitter

Medium: Acrylic

Purpose of Works: Book jackets

Commissioned by: Hippo Books (Imprint) Scolastic Publications

151

John Martin & Artists Ltd.

tel: **071 734 9000**   fax: **071 226 6069**

26 Danbury Street
London
N1 8JU

John Martin & Artists Ltd. were established in 1956 and have since that date dealt with a wide range of commissions from both advertising and publishers including adult and childrens' books. We have forty artists who illustrate many different subjects

We are situated in pleasant premises eight minutes walk from the new Angel tube at Islington and would be pleased to see anyone interested in the work of our artists

152

1: David Templeton (McMillan)
2: Beverly Lees
3: Rebecca Hardy

John Martin & Artists Ltd.

tel: **071 734 9000**   fax: **071 226 6069**

1: **Wayne Glossop**
2: **Cathie Shuttleworth**
3: **David Price (Coronet)**

Martine Gourbalt

tel: **071 431 6130** fax: **071 431 6129**

14 Nassington Road
London NW3 2UD

1: Medium: Colour pencils

Purpose of Work: Book jacket
for *Four Clever Mice*

Commissioned by:
Greenwillow Publishers

2: Medium: Colour pencils

Purpose of Work;
Childrens' book illustration

Martine Gourbalt was born in Paris. After a successful career in Canada in magazine illustration and art direction, she began illustrating childrens' books four years ago, while living in New York. She has since had several books published by Greenwillow Books and other US publishers. She works primarily in colour pencils. She now lives and works in London

Liam O'Farrell

tel: **081 521 9675** fax: **081 521 9675**

262 Hoe Street
Walthamstow
London
E17 3AX

Title: Under Milkwood

Medium: Oil paint & varnish

Purpose of Work: Self-promotion

Kevin Myler

tel: **0922 711778**   fax: **0922 711778**

6 Moore Road
New Invention
Willenhall
West Midlands
WV12 5HD

1:Title: Anatomy of a Healing Hand

Medium: Gouache

Purpose of Work:
AOI Competition (Prizewinner)

Brief: To express the healing potential of dolphins

2: Medium: Gouache

Purpose of Work: Personal project

3: Medium: Coloured pencil

Purpose of Work: Mailshot cover

Commissioned by:
International Management Magazine

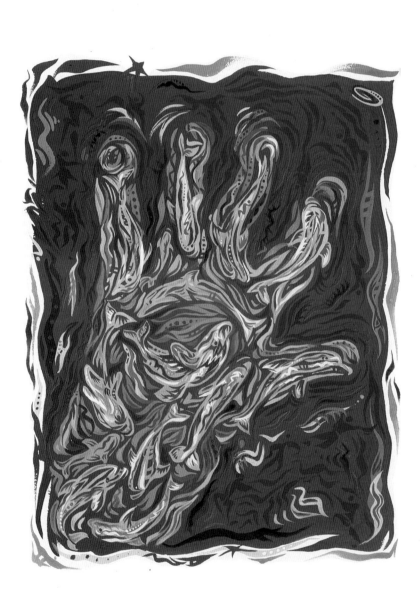

Patricia Moffett

tel: 0865 773868 fax: 0865 773868

103 Campbell Road
Oxford
OX4 3NX

Title: Figures and Majic

Worked so far only in publishing. Enjoy mostly figure work for narrative subjects. Would like to work with light & costume for small theatre at some point

Ian Inniss

tel: **081 961 5092 / 071 794 5196**

32 Hiscocks House
Stilton Crescent
London
NW10 8DD

Mainly conceptual illustrations, essentially
figurative; animals and people

Areas of interest include packaging, editorial,
print & design, publishing and advertising.
However, I am currently working on a childrens'
safety centre, which is proving to be very interesting

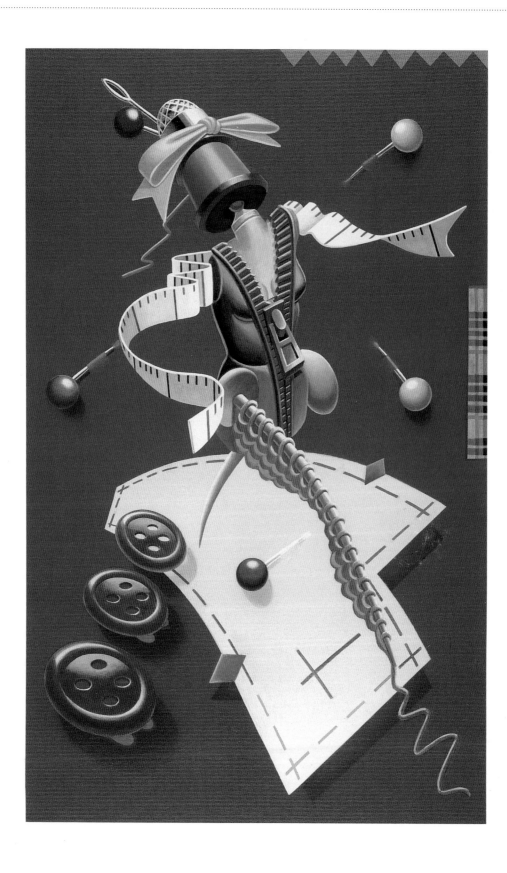

Rory Little

tel: **081 244 7149**   fax: **081 778 6906**

119 Sydenham Park Road
London
SE26 4LP

Title: Arabian Knights

Medium: Watercolour & gouache

Purpose of Work: Self-promotional book illustration

Keith Hodgson Coloured Inc.

tel: **0642 700466**   fax: **0642 701244**

Folly Hill
Skutterskelfe Park
Hutton Rudby
Cleveland
TS15 OJL

Childrens' books, educational and fiction, plus advertising and editorial, for a plethora of clients all sporting a commendable proclivity for the absurd

Media ranges from Airbrush to Apple Mac Quadra with Wacom Tablet, through to a crudely fashioned cheese grater from Czechoslovakia and a pickled walnut called Edith

Sample: Fat Albert's Time Machine....Fat Albert materialises on Planet Aardvark to discover the gentle Gherkin people under sustained attack

160

Shaw Harper

tel: 03967 22642   fax: 03967 23577

The Millstone
7 Bryansford Village
Newcastle
Co. Down
N. Ireland BT33 0PT

A creative director for twenty years and a member of D&AD. Used to panic deadlines, I have worked extensively for advertising, design, books, editorial, calendars, visuals and storyboards

I can work in various styles and mediums, to tight or loose briefs, and for humorous rates!

Clients include: BT, Guinness, TSB, Milk Marketing Board, First Trust Bank, DHSS, Dept. of the Environment and my mum

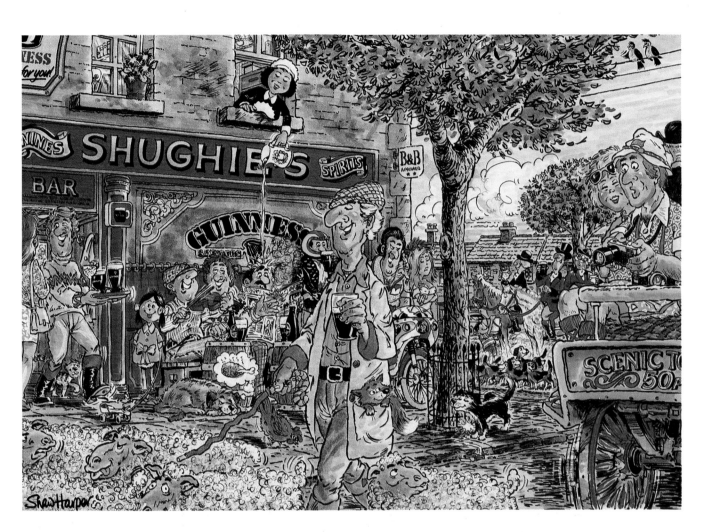

Blair Grant

tel: **0222 667801**   fax: **0222 667801**

1 Clare Road
Riverside
Cardiff
CF1 7QN

A bright quirky style with a hint of humour,
readily adaptable to any briefing requiring
lively characterization. Accepting commissions
for editorial, publishing, advertising and packaging
I also produce cartoon characters and strips

Please ring for further samples or to see the portfolio

162

Lisa Bond

tel: **021 447 7064 / 021 705 3152**

4 Bear Hill
Alvechurch
Birmingham
B48 7JX

1: Medium: Pen & ink

Purpose of Work: 1993 Shell Better Britain Campaign

2: Medium: 3-D collage

Purpose of Work: Linguaphone Childrens' Picture Dictionary

Other clients include: BBC Books, Central TV , Birmingham Tec Council, Homes & Gardens, Punch, The Spectator, Peat Marwick, Country Homes and Interiors and Millward Brown

Try and reach as wide an audience as possible.

You don't have to be a patient to help hospital wildlife.

Wasteland can become a valuable home to wildlife.

Support can be found close to home.

Interview local residents.

Ingrid Darracott

tel: **071 254 2856**   fax: **071 241 6049**

Agent:

début art
52 Barbauld Road
London N16 0ST

1: Brief: Aquarius Horoscope

Commissioned by: YOU Magazine

2: Commissioned by:
Hall & Towse Construction

Ingrid specialises in making illustrations using her own hand-made papers.
She paints and collages onto the paper amongst other techniques

Previous clients include: Freshfields International Law, Hall & Towse
Construction, Banking Technology Magazine, YOU Magazine, The Wigmore Hall,
Decca Records, Creative Review, Micro-Decision Magazine, Acorn User
Magazine, Victor Gollancz Publishing and Walker Publishing

Grimwood

tel: **071 240 8925**   fax: **071 836 1177**

Central Illustration Agency
36 Wellington Street
London
WC2E 7BD

Joanna Kemp

tel: 0223 321677

61 Mulberry Close
Cambridge
CB4 2AS

Medium: Watercolours and watercolour pencils

Purpose of Work: Speculative

Brief: Based on Lewis Carrol's *Alice In Wonderland*

I like to work on fantasy subjects, which include animals, both real and mythical, and can adapt my work to suit requirements

A series of my paintings are to be reproduced as postcards by Wizart, which include dragon, mermaid and unicorn subjects. I have also worked on greetings cards

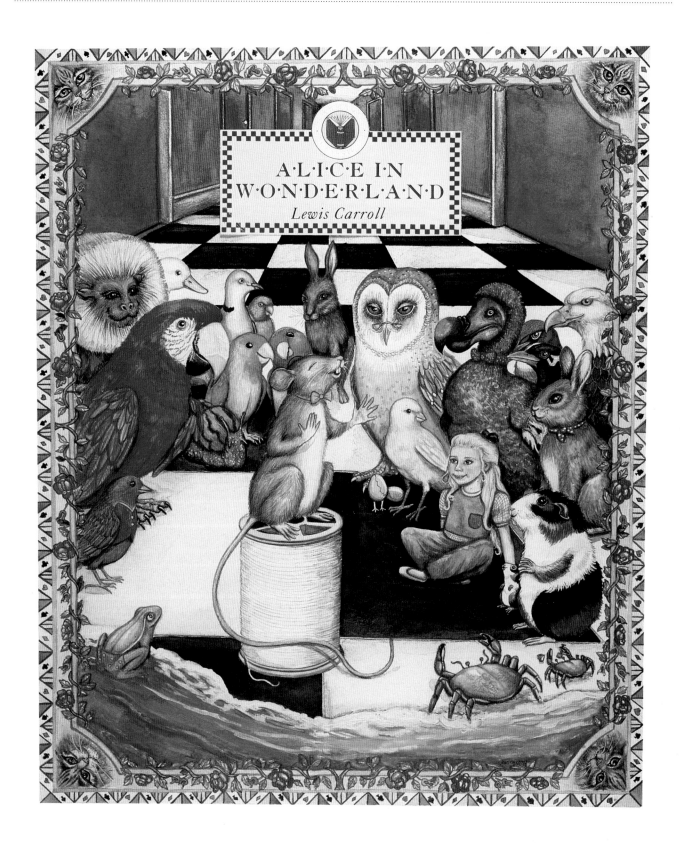

Mark Thomas

tel: **071 240 8925**   fax: **071 836 1177**

Central Illustration Agency
36 Wellington Street
London
WC2E 7BD

SATURDAY DECEMBER 5 1992

THE TIMES

Saturday Review

TRAMP ON THE RUN

The untold story
of Charles Chaplin
and J. Edgar Hoover

•

Plus: Sam Fox revealed

Claire Davies

Cuckoo Lodge
Gallow Hill
Wells-next-the-Sea
Norfolk
NR23 1SE

Agent: Central Illustration Agency
36 Wellington Street
London WC2E 7BD

tel: 071 240 8925
fax: 071 836 1177

Medium: Watercolour

Purpose of Work: Self-promotion

Claire Davies is an experienced illustrator specialising in publishing and packaging. She works in watercolour, pencils and pastel. Clients include Harper Collins, Penguin, Pan, The BBC, Boots, Sainsburys and Marks and Spencers. She has also been commissioned by European packaging designers

Maggie Ramage

tel: **041 334 4265**   fax: **041 334 4265**

72 Highburgh Road
Glasgow
G12 9EN
Scotland

Title: Comfort & Joy

Medium: Watercolour

Purpose of Work: Editorial

Brief: Young widow spending first Christmas alone is befriended by grandson of elderly neighbour

Commissioned by: Annabel magazine
Published by DC Thompson through Allied Artists

I specialise in figurative work in watercolour, gouache & acrylic. Although I have clients in editorial and book publishing, most of my work consists of privately commissioned portraits. In this illustration, I have used family and friends as models

Kay Smith

tel: **0473 718143**   fax: **0473 718143**

751 Woodbridge Road
Ipswich
Suffolk
IP4 4NB

Title: For Love or Carrots

Purpose of Work: Self-portrait

If you need detailed and
decorative work, I'm your illustrator

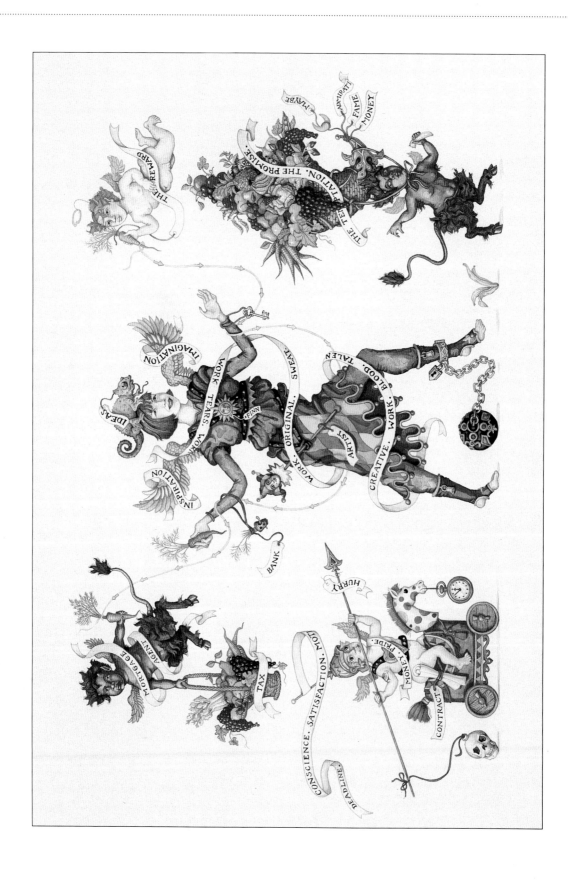

John Norris Wood & Kevin Dean

John Norris Wood
The Brook Dewhurst Lane
Wadhurst Sussex TN5 6QE

tel: 0892 782606
fax: 0892 782606

Kevin Dean
154 Kennington Park Road
London SE11 4DJ

tel: 071 793 9972
fax: 071 793 9972

'Jungles' and 'Rivers & Lakes' (from the *Nature Hide & Seek* series) are devised and written by John Norris Wood and illustrated jointly with Kevin Dean. The first two books, chosen by The American Association for The Advancement of Science as Childrens' Science Books of the Year, have sold 350 000 copies worldwide. They feature large gatefold panoramas, showing creatures camouflaged within their environment. Both artists are active conservationists, intimately familiar with the habitats they illustrate

Spike Gerrell

tel: 081 340 7488   fax: 081 340 7488

11 Mountview Road
London
N4 4SS

You'd usually get a voluminous list of impressive clients here, but I'll dispense with that. Suffice to say that you'll get your colour, tone or line artwork to whatever unreasonable deadline you have to work to and very lovely it will be too

Vale & Betts

tel: **081 691 4641**   fax: **081 691 4641**

27 Wilshaw House
Creekside
London
SE8 4SF

Simon Ritchie

tel: **0371 830804**   fax: **0371 830804**

46 Newbiggen Street
Thaxted
Essex
CM6 2QR

I cut my teeth in advertising and understand deadlines and briefs

My work covers all sorts from black and white diagrams to figure work and architectural perspectives from flat plans. I also imitate, pastiche and caricature. *Give me a ring*

174

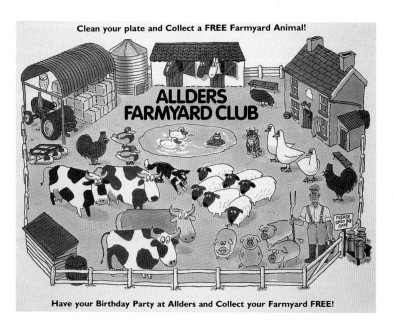

Bill Reid

tel: 031 551 3354   fax: 031 551 1073

48 Connaught Place
Edinburgh
EH6 4RN

1: Title: Butler

Medium: Ink

Purpose of Work: Self-promotional

2: Title: Car

Medium: Inks

Purpose of Work: Self-promotional

3: Title: Loch Ness Monster

Medium: Ink

Purpose of work: One of a series of illustrations on Scottish themes for the Reid Partnership.

L O C H N E S S

Paul Davis

tel: 071 739 6233   fax: 071 613 2341

Studio 205
2nd Floor
134-146 Curtain Road
London EC2A 3AR

Agent: début art
52 Barbauld Road
London N16 0ST

tel: 071 254 2856
fax: 071 241 6049

Title: Mapping the Millenium - The X / Y Axis

Commissioned by: Blueprint magazine

Other clients include: BP, Royal Mail, Barclays, BBC, Warner Bros, Virgin, ICL, Legal & General, 3i Investments, Bloomsbury, New Scientist, Chiat & Day, Kellogs, Centaur, Redwood, VNU, MTV, GQ, Docklands Guide and WH Smiths

Jo Fernihough

tel: **071 585 2558**

26B Manchuria Road
Clapham
London
SW11 6AE

Purpose of Work: Brochure cover 1993 - 94

Brief: Media Futures

Commissioned by: The Henley Centre

Jon Hamilton

tel: **081 968 7481**   fax: **081 968 7481**

207b Chevening Road
Queens Park
London
NW6 6DT

Title: Portrait of the Dalai Lama

Commissioned by: *Elle* Magazine

Colours influenced by the Dalai Lama's robes, images surrounding show events from his life

I photograph all work myself onto 5 x 4 transparencies and provide detailed line drawing roughs. Work is provided in a short space of time

Clients include: The Body Shop, Conran Design, British Telecom, Royal Academy of Art, Jonathan Cape, New Scientist, PC Direct, Marie Claire, J. Walter Thompson, Chiat Day and Bravo

Matthew Cooper

tel: **071 254 2856**

103 College Road
Kensal Green
London NW10 5EY

Agent: Début Art
52 Barbauld Road
London N10 0ST

tel: 081 969 4832
fax: 071 241 6049

Brief: To create the cover image for the entry brochure of an award scheme around the theme of Water

Commissioned by: Band and Brown for the *Prince's Trust*

Other Clients include: Wolff Olins, Vintage Publishing, British Telecom, Domino Records, Heinemann Publishing, New Scientist Magazine, Asda, Penguin Publishing, Longmans

Lawrence Zeegen

tel: **071 739 7765**   fax: **071 613 2341**

Big Orange
2nd Floor
Back Building
150 Curtain Road
London EC2A 3AR

Title: We're Looking for
People Who Like to Draw

Medium: Drawing & mixed media

Toby Morison

tel: 071 739 7765   fax: 071 613 2341

Big Orange
2nd Floor
Back Building
150 Curtain Road
London EC2A 3AR

Medium: Acrylic on paper

Purpose of Work: Editorial

Commissioned by: Mark Porter
Evening Standard Magazine

Ray Belletty

tel: **071 739 7765**   fax: **071 613 2341**

Big Orange
2nd Floor
Back Building
150 Curtain Road
London EC2A 3AR

Title: Vodka

Medium: Acrylic

Purpose of Work: Editorial

Commissioned by: Helen Bratby *Tatler*

Lara Harwood

tel: **081 549 9712**

Big Orange 2nd Floor
Back Building
150 Curtain Road
London EC2A 3AR

tel: **071 739 7765**   fax: **071 613 2341**

Title: Vitamins & Pregnancy

Commissioned by: Cathy Caldwell &
Caroline Harper *Elle* magazine

Dan Williams

tel: **071 739 7765** fax: **071 613 2341**

Big Orange
2nd Floor
Back Building
150 Curtain Road
London EC2A 3AR

Medium: Acrylic on board

Commissioned by: Anne Braybon
International Management

184

Sarah McMenemy

tel: **071 739 7765** fax: **071 613 2341**

Big Orange
2nd Floor
Back Building
150 Curtain Road
London EC2A 3AR

Agency: The Artworks

Title: Fountain, Dorsoduro, Venice

Medium: Collage & mixed media

From an exhibition of personal work about
Italy held at The Artworks Gallery

Andrew Lovell

tel: **071 739 7765**   fax: **071 613 2341**

Big Orange
2nd Floor
Back Building
150 Curtain Road
London EC2A 3AR

Title: Super Tailor

Medium: Printmaking, collage & photocopying

From a series of work inspired by travels in India

Jason Ford

Big Orange
2nd Floor
Back Building
150 Curtain Road
London EC2A 3AR

tel: **071 739 7765** fax: **071 613 2341**

Title: The Space Race

Medium: Acrylic & ink on board

Purpose of Work: Editorial

Commissioned by: Jim McClure Airline
Business Magazine Reed Business Publishing

Clients include: Saatchi & Saatchi, WH Smiths,
The Sunday Times Magazine and Mercury

Darrell Rees

Big Orange
2nd Floor
Back Building
150 Curtain Road
London EC2A 3AR

tel: **071 739 7765**   fax: **071 613 2341**

Title: Man Maid

Medium: Collage / montage

Purpose of Work: Editorial

Brief: To accompany an article about domestic robots

Commissioned by: *The Times Saturday Magazine*

Blaise Thompson

tel: **071 739 7765**   fax: **071 613 2341**

Big Orange
2nd Floor
Back Building
150 Curtain Road
London EC2A 3AR

Title: The Oval, Kennington

Medium: Mixed media & collage on paper

![The Oval, Kennington — a mixed media and collage artwork depicting a cricket scoreboard with numbers and text including "No 7 TOTAL", "WICKETS 6", "BOWLER 12", "SURREY", "OVERS 24", "LAST WKT", "BONUS POINTS", "INNS 2"]

Anthea Whitworth

tel: 0279 442099

44 Pottersfield
Harlow
Essex
CM17 9BZ

Title: Bliss

Medium: Coloured pencils

Purpose of Work: For a childrens' book I am working
on entitled *Patrick's Peculiar Pyjamas*. This is a
personal project which I hope to get published

Ian Pollock

14 Crompton Road
Maccelsfield
Cheshire
SK11 8DS

tel: **0625 426205** fax: **0625 500617**

Title:
The Pleasure of Reading

Medium:
Watercolour, ink and gouache

Commissioned by: Nick Thirkell of *Carroll, Dempsey & Thirkell Design Consultants* on behalf of WH Smith and Bloomsbury Publishing Ltd. for *'The Pleasure of Reading'* edited by Antonia Fraser. The illustration accompanies the contribution by J.G.Ballard

Ashley Potter

tel: **071 639 9695**

23 Collinson House
Peckham Park Road
London
SE15 6UU

Title: Tattooed Swimmer - Captain

Medium: Acrylic

Purpose of Work: Character and costume design for a Post Office television commercial

Commissioned by: Mario Cavelli *Pizzaz Pictures*

For other examples of work, see Images 7 - 15, European Illustration 9 & 11, Illustration Now, Contact 8 & Contact 9 Illustrators Agents.

Clients include: Penguin, Picador, Faber & Faber, Sphere, New Scientist, Radio Times, The Observer, The Sunday Times, GQ, Esquire, Tatler, Island Records, Decca, JWT, HHC & L, SPCD and GGT

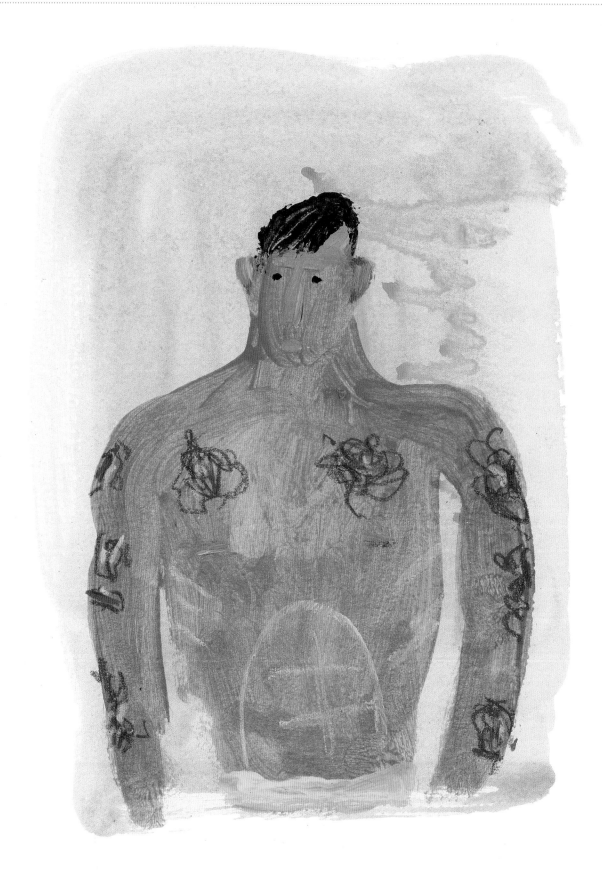

Jean-Paul Tibbles

tel: **071 240 8925**   fax: **071 836 1177**

**Central Illustration Agency
36 Wellington Street
London
WC2E 7BD**

Working mainly in oils, Jean-Paul Tibbles
regularly receives commissions from major
advertising agencies, design groups and
publishers internationally

Britta Teckentrup

tel: 071 241 6327 / 071 704 8797   **fax: 071 241 6327**

14 Horton Road
Dalston
London E8

Title: The Marie Claire Love Tapes

Medium: Collage

Purpose of Work: Editorial

Brief: To design an image representing a one-month affair

Commissioned by: Suzanne Sykes *Marie Claire*

Other clients include: Vogue, Elle, The South Bank Centre, Paperchase, ABC All Books for Children, Metropolis Design Consultancy, Hot Graphics, The Creative Handbook ('First Choice' Section), and various others

194

Tracey Ramsdale

tel: **0332 45448**   fax: **0332 45448**

84 Sherwin Street
Derby
DE22 1GN

Medium: Lino print & paper collage

My work has been commisioned by a variety of clients including: Anchor Housing Association, Heinemann International, Oxford University Press, Boots plc, Kentish Property, Merseyside Maritime Museum and Capital Publishing

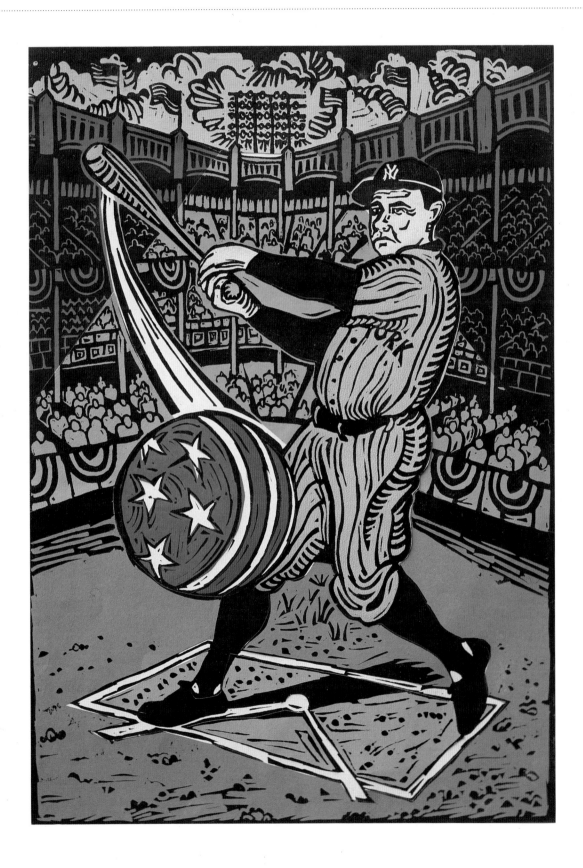

Simon Henwood

tel: **081 806 0744**

Agency: Gotham Art & Literary Agency Inc. New York

tel: 212 989 2737
fax: 212 645 7731

Title: Alice

Purpose of Work: Illustration from an upcoming book and exhibition: a new edition of Alice in Wonderland which re-establishes the appeal of Alice for anyone from 8 to 80 years old

Title: Metropolis

Purpose of Work: Illustrations from a book and film by the artist

UK clients include: Pan Books, Macmillan, Harper Collins, Oxford University Press, The Bodley Head, Linguaphone and National Magazine Co.

US clients include Farra, Straus & Giroux, the Putnam and Grosset Group, William Morrow, Atheneum, Simon & Schuster and the New York Times

Gary Bates

Agent: début art
52 Barbauld Road
London N16 0ST

tel: 071 254 2856
fax: 071 241 6049

Recent clients include:
Independent on Sunday, LWT, British Gas,
Co-op Bank, Penguin Books, The Observer,
Tatler, BBC Music Magazine, The Design
Council and The Financial Times

Anne Magill

tel: **081 293 1304**   fax: **081 293 1268**

Agent: Guitty Talberg
142A Greenwich High Road
Greenwich
London SE10 8NN

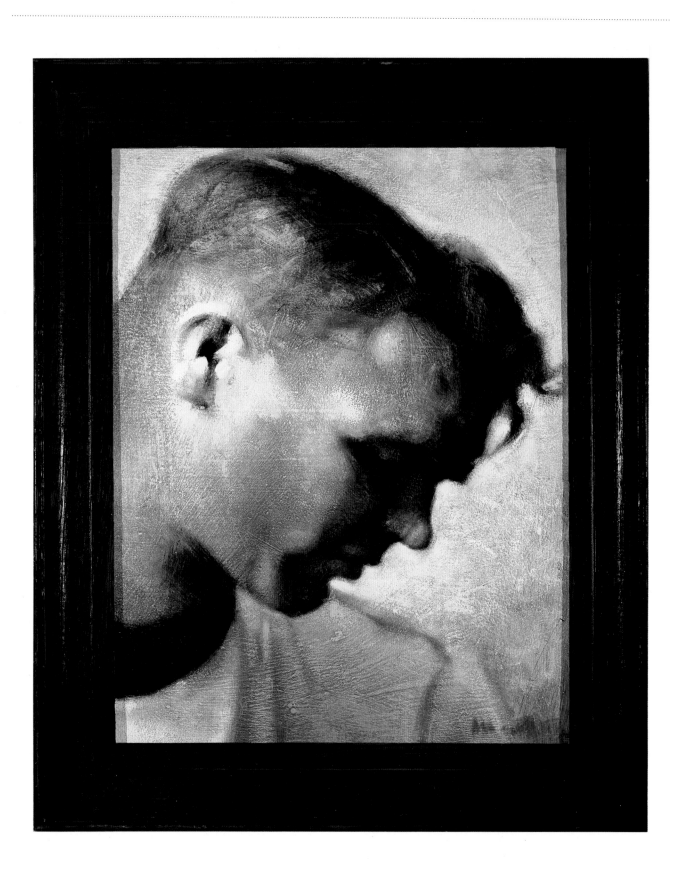

Helen Manning

tel: **081 293 1304**   fax: **081 293 1268**

Agent: Guitty Talberg
142A Greenwich High Road
Greenwich
London SE10 8NN

Jayne Morris

tel: **081 293 1304** fax: **081 293 1268**

Agent: Guitty Talberg
142A Greenwich High Road
Greenwich
London SE10 8NN

Paul Schofield   Gillian Martin

tel: **081 293 1304**   fax: **081 293 1268**

Agent: Guitty Talberg
142A Greenwich High Road
Greenwich
London SE10 8NN

Morse Design & Illustration
Mohsen John Modaberi
78 Hanley Road
London
N4 3DR

Book

Advertising

Print & Design

Information & Technology

Unpublished Student

Unpublished Professional

Professional

Newcomers

Claire M. Sweeney

tel: **0232 682250**

43 Ethel Street
Belfast
BT9 7FT
Co. Antrim
N. Ireland

Title (1): Taurus

Medium: Water-based ink

Purpose of Work:
Horoscope for a magazine
Self-commissioned

Title (2): Angela Carter's
Nights at the Circus

Medium: Water-based ink

Purpose of Work: Book cover

I have a passion for ancient cultures, particularly my own Celtic tradition. I enjoy colour and texture, finding inspiration in African & European primitive art

Rhona Garvin

tel: 071 582 8134

50 Crewdson Road
London
SW9 0LJ

I produce mono-prints, etchings and pen & ink
drawings in a lively and idiosynchratic style.
My interests lie mainly in the areas of editorial,
travel, greeting cards and childrens' illustration

Helen Entwistle

14 Elterwater Crescent
Barrow-in-Furness
Cumbria
LA14 4PH

3-D is only one aspect of my work. I am also inspired by cinemagraphic lighting to portray an atmosphere, thereby creating a bizarre mini-theatre. My passion for these techniques recently took me further into the exploration of the moving image. Using the 3-D characters from one of my illustrations, I have made a short animated film. I am now looking to counterpoint my illustrations with a filmic language

Alex Kurtagić

120 Lexham Gardens
London
W8 6JE

Title: Supermodel Serial Killer

Medium: Colour pencils

Purpose of Work: Self-promotion

Brief: A perfectly average citizen has taken it upon itself to brutally exterminate the deleterious icons that perpetuate the beauty myth.

A tribute to Naomi Wolf

Andrea Farmer

tel: **0708 222403**

8 Fairfield Avenue
Upminster
Essex
RM14 3AY

Title: Scorpio - The Detective

Medium: Acrylic

Purpose of Work:
Entry for Elle Horoscope Talent Contest 1993

Lisa Aldridge

tel: **081 993 5016**

Flat 4
54 Twyford Avenue
London
W3 9QB

Colour image: Part of a college project to
look at the possible future of British game shows

Black & White image: A personal project for my portfolio
looking at the relationship between pets and their owners

Graduate of Norfolk Institute of Art & Design 1992

Joanne Spengler

tel: c/o AOI **071 631 1510**

Title: Pisces - The Dreamer

Medium: Mixed media

Purpose of Work: College project Book jacket

Jonathan Williams

tel: 031 226 5754   fax: 031 225 3699

Studio 6
Castlecliff Workshops
25 Johnston Terrace
Edinburgh
EH1 2NH

Title: Straining out a Gnat,
Swallowing a Camel *(St. Matthew 23: 23,24)*

The Bible has meant an enormous amount to me. It takes the
confusion and uncertainty of life, condenses it into a few words
and gives back the truth. Times change, but human nature
and the truth about human nature, doesn't

My work attempts to reconcile a changing
experience of life with an unchanging truth

Naomi Stolow

tel: **081 346 3693**

46B Holdenhurst Avenue
Finchley
London N12 OJB

Lynda Jane Collins

tel: 0435 830632

Byschool
Rushlake Green
Heathfield
East Sussex
TN21 9QN

Title: Food For Thought

Medium: Inks

I work in both colour and black & white and use the rich vibrant colours of inks to produce small minimal images

My black & white images are simple monoprints making use of tone and texture. I usually interpret text relating to / commenting on current social topics

See also Images 18, Newcomers section

David Swift

The Elms
off Moor Road
Strelley
Nottingham
NG8 6NH

My interests are based in natural objects studied
in close detail and I often integrate other shapes
and colours into my work. I work in pen & ink,
mixed media, paper engineering and pop-up design.
Thanks to a background in graphic design,
I can also integrate calligraphy into my work

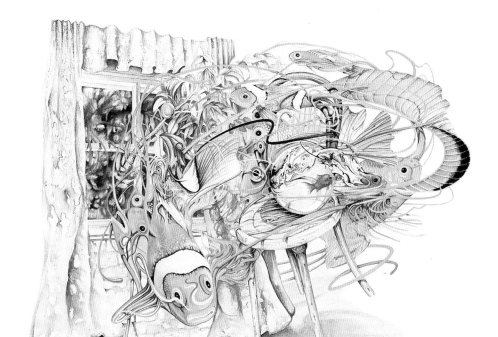

Jenny Bidgood

tel: **0884 860349**   fax: **0884 860349**

23 West Street
Witheridge
Tiverton
Devon EX16 8AA

Title: The Mole's Birthday Party

Medium: Scraperboard with liquid acrylic

Recent work includes educational books and greetings cards. I have a particular interest in images from country life and history

Highly Commended in the Readers Digest Young Illustrator of the Year 1989

Matthew A. Williams

tel: **0865 64178**

7 Trafford Road
Headington
Oxford
OX3 8BD

Working mainly in oils and watercolour, encompassing a broad range of landscape, figurative and architectural subject matter, I am happy to receive commissions from all areas of illustration

I admire the old impressionist masters and have a keen interest in contemporary impressionist art and illustration and in old Victorian photography.

Ivan Smith

tel: **0732 354840**

17 Rose Street
Tonbridge
Kent
TN9 2BN

Mainly figurative work in pencils & acrylic.

My interests include making and acting in videos and science fiction, and I have illustrated for the Blakes 7 fan club, Horizon

As well as submitting work to various sci-fi publications I have had some success drawing caricatures for the local paper and selling paintings of the area

Natasha Webber

tel: 0494 88 2651

Framers Cottage
Plot 2 Marlow Road
Lane End
nr. High Wycombe
Bucks HP14 3JP

My work is often water-colour based, using other media to enhance it. I am inspired by different techniques and textural effects which I often find in surface patterns and experiment using different materials

One of my greatest enjoyments is integrating type into my illustrations. Calligraphy allows me to create my own visual language

218

Gemini

POSITIVE:- Bright & quick witted Capable of doing many different things. Open-minded. Governed more by mind than Emotions. Never short of Imagi-nation. Good talker. Often center of Attraction.

NEGATIVE:- Does too many things at once. Easily distracted. Finds it too boring to become serious. Some are never dependable. Can be sharp tongued and inconsiderate.

...MERCURY...
Planet closest to the sun. It represents the capacity to understand the desires of your own will

David Darby

tel: **081 366 7413**

97 Brigadier Hill
Enfield
Middlesex
EN2 0NL

Purpose of Work:
Self-promotional college project

Student of Graphic Design & Illustration

Working at present as a freelance
designer in pre-production

Catherine Foottit

tel: **0223 316146**

5 Leys Avenue
Cambridge
CB4 2AN

Graduate of Bath College of Higher
Education B.A. (Hons) Graphic Design
specialising in Illustration.

My work is two-dimensionally observed and is
achieved mainly through the mixed media of watercolour,
pencil crayon and acrylic. When working on a brief I
look predominantly to live material for reference.

My style is particularly suitable for packaging work or
any other brief where observed drawing is needed

220

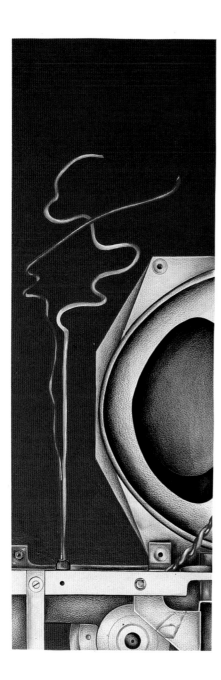
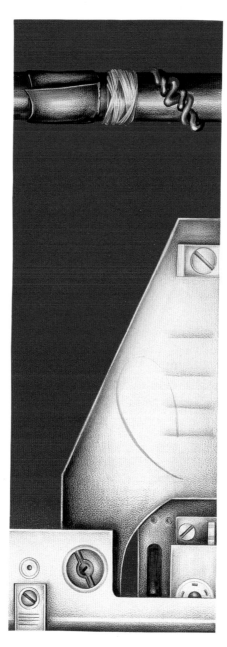

Simon Christopher Smith

tel: **0602 261097**   fax: **0602 414763**

1 Calstock Road
Woodthorpe
Nottingham
NG5 4FH

My style is 3-Dimensional, employing a wide range of materials, the essence of each piece being reliant on line work

Along with publishing, advertising and editorial work, my style is ideal for use in exhibition and window displays; some of my most recent work was a series of seven window displays for Ted Baker Ltd.

Roberto Feo

tel: **071 732 6614 / 071 252 5761**

26 Northfield House
Peckham Park Road
London
SE15 6TL

Title: Love in the Time of Cholera

Medium: Acrylic on paper

Purpose of Work: Book jacket

Joe Stoneman

tel: **0252 795118**

The Stables
Dochenfield Farm
Frensham
Surrey
GU10 3EF

Medium: Oil on canvas

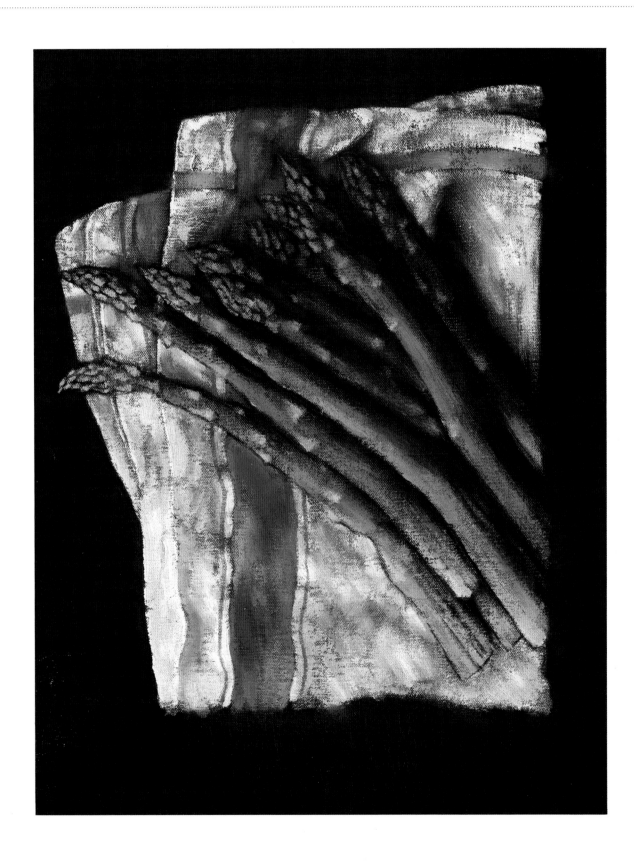

Vernon Yabsley

tel: 081 341 1763

86A Falkland Road
Hornsey
London
N8 0NP

Title: Body Building Vanity

Medium: Silkscreen & etching

Purpose of Work: Self-promotional

Brief: To satirize today's steroid pumping scene

I like to work with various printing methods as it forces you to get straight to the point

Claire Loder

tel: **0223 891826**   fax: **0223 891854**

38 South Road
Great Abington
Cambridge
CB1 6AU

Title: The Travelling Boy
and the Stay-at-Home Bird

Medium: Watercolour

Purpose of Work:
Self-initiated illustration for a play on Radio 5

I also combine this medium with collage,
having a penchant for the unprized photo-copier,
working to a range of briefs particularly editorial
or freely within a greetings card format

David Grimwood

tel: 0522 530167

30 Wills Close
Lincoln
LN1 3LA

Title: Dyslexia

Commissioned by:
Lincolnshire College of Art

I am entering the second year of a degree course
at Kingston University and will continue to pursue
my goals of improved draughtmanship and painting

I am interested mainly in social / philosophical aspects
of our society and would like to attract commissions in
the editorial sphere

Suzanne Breeze

tel: 0323 737423

83 Susans Road
Eastbourne
East Sussex

Title: The Puppet Master

Medium: Oil, although I usually
use acrylic for my editorial work

Brief: To create an illustration for
Angela Carter's novel, *The Magic Toyshop*

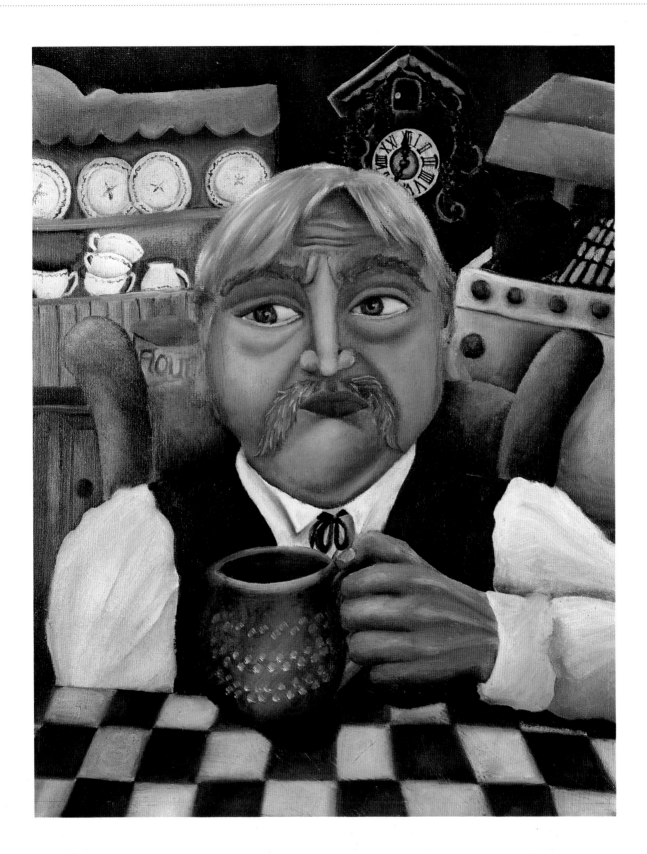

Alison Barratt

tel: **081 340 8557**   fax: **081 340 8557**

Title: Agriculture & Industry
in India since Independence

Medium: Pastel

Purpose of Work: Book covers

Commissioned by: T.V. Sathyamurthy
University of York Indian Studies

Client: Oxford University Press in India

228

Janine Esmund

tel: 0372 725954

56 Albert Road
Epsom
Surrey
KT17 4EH

Brief: To design a cover for a mail order catalogue for books about design

This brought together many elements of design together in the form of collage with hand rendered type, which are special interests of mine. I also like to include simple line drawings in pen & ink, exploring the qualities of line, but generally work quite loosely with mixed media

Andrew Steward

tel: **021 427 5020**

46 Vicarage Road
Harborne
Birmingham
B17 0SP

Purpose of Work: Brochure cover for the Design Council, Books by Post

It depicts a person physically and visually digesting the the books, causing his head to explode due to a combination of excitement and knowledge

I invite the viewer to interpret my illustrations in his own way, and enjoy depicting socially relevent statements

230

Fiona Fraser

tel: 072 273302

Swans Drift
Great Durnford
Salisbury
Wiltshire
SP4 6AY

For many years I have worked as a graphic designer. Projects include Andrew Grima Jewellery Shop (international House Style), Edgley Aeronautics (the Optica Aeroplane, complete livery and House Style) and Paris and Farnborough Airshow stands

More recent jobs include architectural and food and wine illustration, calligraphy, 'Offshoots' gardening illustration for the Christmas issue of Homes and Gardens and 1994 cards for Camden Graphics

Suzanne Ewart

tel: **081 948 4462**

33 Windsor Road
Kew Gardens
Richmond
Surrey
TW9 2EJ

Title: Easy Harvest

Medium: Gouache

Isabel Rayner

tel: **0636 702837**

c/o 3 Elm Avenue
Newark
Notts
NG24 1SE

Purpose of Work: Self promotional

Brief: Book jacket for
EM Forster's *A Passage To India*

I work in pencil crayons & line / watercolour wash
with emphasis on strong lighting

My work is stylized realism and my subjects include
landscapes, people, buildings, interiors and designs

Andrew Selby

tel: **0279 731452**   fax: **0279 731452**

9 Perryfield
Matching Green
Essex
CM17 0PY

Illustrations in watercolour for editorial,
publishing & advertising purposes

Clients include:
HHL Publishing, Butterworths,
IPC, Emap & BBC

Carol Mitchell

tel: **0634 865875**

112 Chestnut Avenue
Walderslade
Chatham
Kent
ME5 9BG

Title (1): Alsace

Medium: Watercolour & coloured pencil

Purpose of Work: Self-promotion

Brief: To encapsulate the Alsace region in a single illustration for a travel / good food guide for France

Title (2): Mexicana

Medium: Watercolour & coloured pencils

Purpose of Work: Self-promotion

Brief: To illustrate a menu cover for a Mexican restaurant

Anna Bisset

tel: **081 503 2174**

54 Brettenham Road
Walthamstow
London
E17 5BA

Title: A Chemical Reaction

Brief: Created as a wedding card for two scientists

Graduate of Bath Academy of Art (B.A.Hons). Having had experience in a wide range of media including three dimensional work, I am now concentrating solely on illustration and looking forward to tight deadlines and interesting briefs.

Runner-up in Elle Talent Contest 1993 (Aquarius)

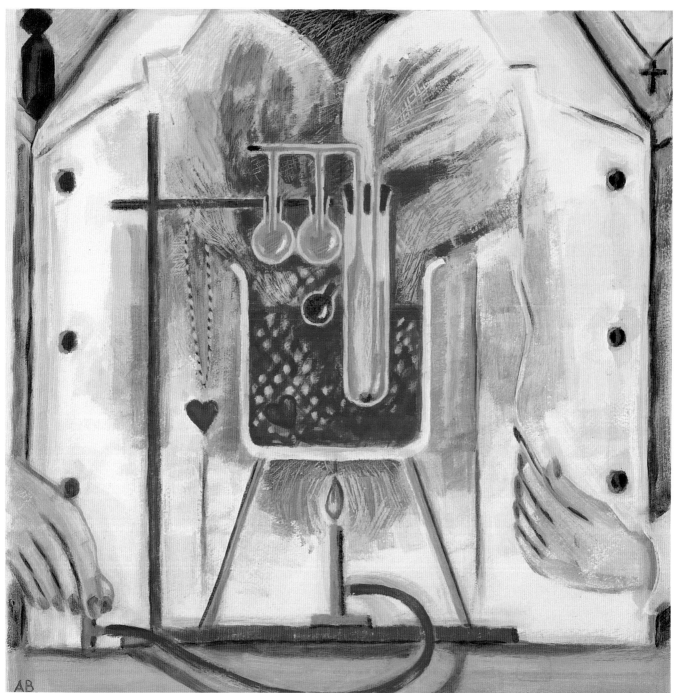

Philippa Sutherland

tel: 071 326 4542

86 Strathleven Road
London
SW2 5LE

Title: Sinking Slowly

Medium: Acrylic & collage

Purpose of Work: Personal project

Brief: One of a series of images on industrial decline

Philippa Sutherland

86 Strathleven Road
London
SW2 5LE

Title: Sinking Slowly

Medium: Acrylic & collage

Purpose of Work: Personal project

Brief: One of a series of images on industrial decline

Colin Pells

tel: **0494 726449**

15 Lexham Gardens
Amersham
Bucks
HP6 5JP

Working in alleyds gives the creative flexibility and quick drying reliability needed in my painting

My subject matter varies considerably but I am keen to develop ideas for commissions as the conceptual is particularly suited to my style and process of illustration

238

Lucy Bristow

tel: **081 947 9815**   fax: **081 944 5335**

42B Queens Road
Wimbledon
London
SW19 8LR

Title: Bedtime Stories: are our dreams trying to tell us something?

Medium: Oil pastel

Purpose of Work:
Magazine article illustration

Brief: To accompany an article about the meaning of dreams

Commissioned by: Nikki Bowden *Ms London*

Bharat Mistry

tel: c/o AOI **071 631 1510**

37 Hartington Road
Leicester

Medium: Watercolour, inks & pastels

Size: 255mm x 370mm

Brief: To express the ever-increasing variety of witty lager & beer advertisements on TV

Having worked for magazines and design groups, my work is widely recognised for its conceptual, witty and busy imagery

Sandra Andrews

tel: **081 693 4315**   fax: **081 693 4315**

115 Crystal Palace Road
East Dulwich
London
SE22 9ES

Recent clients include:
Radio Times, Observer Magazine, New
Scientist, New Statesman and British Council

Annemarie Huck

tel: **081 986 5589**   fax: **081 986 5589**

1 Church Crescent
London E9 7DH

Mat Edwards

tel: **0782 723286**   fax: **0782 715857**

51 Scot Hay Road
Alsagers Bank
Stoke-on-Trent
ST7 8BW

Training and working as a ceramic repro artist taught me many skills, such as reproducing artwork, pencil drawing, camera and film work, ink drawing and airbrushing. My speciality is producing imaginary high-detailed artwork, usually painted in gouache and ink. I also develop collector ceramic plates from the original and have been producing large detailed murals

243

Julia Clay

tel: 0453 885560 **fax: 0453 731060**

High Beaches
Briscombe
Nr Stroud
Gloucester
GL5 2FBN

Title: Amazonian Rain Forest

Medium
Gouache and watercolour

Purpose of work: Backdrop for a museum exhibition showing fauna and flora of the Amazonian rain forest

Neil Gray

tel: **071 274 3510**   fax: **071 274 3510**

16 Grove Park
Camberwell
London
SE5 8LH

Highly original sculptural illustration in two and three dimensions, created quickly and accurately to order

From travelogues to Sonic the Hedgehog, editorials to an altogether more rounded caricature. Illuminated backdrops and enlightened models supplied camera-ready or as transparencies

index

NIPPIN' PIPPINS? (4,6)

SF243A

13 mg TAR
SMOKING WHEN PREC
Health Departme

NICOTINE
NT HARMS YOUR BABY
ef Medical Officers

CREATE TIME FOR ESSENTIAL READING

CREATIVE REVIEW

October 1993 £2.50
A Centaur Publication

ROJAN HORSE PUBLISHING

order form

Further copies of *Images 18* can be ordered at a reduced price of £12 plus £3 postage & packing direct from the publisher.

Name:_____

Address:_____

_____

Postcode:_____

tel:_____ **fax:**_____

Number of copies:_____

Total enclosed £_____

Send to:

Trojan Horse Publishing

1 Church Crescent

London E9 7DH

tel: 081 986 5589

fax: 081 986 5589

Cheques payable to '*Images*' – Trojan Horse Publishing Allow 12 working days for delivery